IN MY SISTER'S SHOES
Essays of Inspiration and Encouragement for Women

Jetola E. Anderson-Blair

In My Sister's Shoes, Essays of Inspiration and Encouragement
for Women
Copyright © Jetola E. Anderson-Blair 1999
ISBN 0-9673644-0-X
Library of Congress Catalog Card Number: 99-93463
Jacket art by Juanita Cole Howard
Author Photograph by Jovan Video/Photo

Published by
©**Cross Keys Publishing**
PO Box 752026
Houston, TX 77275
Web site: http://www.pageturner.net/crosskeys

Printed in the United States of America by

MORRIS PUBLISHING
3212 East Highway 30
Kearney, NE 68847
800-650-7888

Dedications

This book is dedicated to the memory of my grandmother,
Mrs. Florence Amanda Barrett
1907-1995

and to my husband, Trevor Anthony Blair, "I Prayed For You."

The Author and her Grandmother

Acknowledgments

Above all, I thank God for the valleys He's brought me through and the lessons I have learned from each experience. I also thank Him for putting strong women in my life to encourage me on my journey.

I also extend a special "thank you" to all my sisters who have encouraged me to "write it down" and have prayed me back from the brink of many a cliff, through my fears, through my tears, through the years. You all know that I've "been there and back" and have a story or two to tell.

Thank you for believing in me when doubt hovered like a cloud. Thank you for celebrating the triumphs, and for being my rock during the rough times. Thank you for holding me up when I fell and couldn't get up. Thanks for the shoulders to cry on, the hankies to cry in and the kicks in the pants. Thank you for knowing which one I needed and, most of all, thank you for never saying "I told you so."

My mother and my aunts
Terolyn Black
Pamela Brown
Megan Diliberto
Katrina Grider
Regina Kirkland
Rhona Richardson
Jinni Rock
Mondell Sealy
H. D. Woodson
Janice Wright
The AKEBA Divas
My ACC Sisterhood
My FCBC Sharing Circle
The Good Book Club
The Houston Chapter of the NBMBAA
Sisters With Books
Anika and the Staff at the Shrine of the Black Madonna

To Pastor Terry Woodson, thank you for your spiritual guidance.

Introduction

It seems that somehow whenever a bunch of women get together, there is always a subgroup that ends up around the kitchen table, swapping war stories on relationships, work, family, and life in general. For some reason, it seems I usually end up a part of such groups. As I shared my personal anecdotes and observations, these women always encouraged me to write them down. I finally took their advice and the result is *In My Sister's Shoes.*

This book was written for every woman who has ever made bad choices and stubbed her toe or fallen down in the game of life. Sometimes when we are fighting our demons or going through our wilderness experiences, we are convinced that we are the only person to have walked this road. It is my hope that *In My Sister's Shoes* will help you to realize that others have been there before you and survived, and you will too. If it helps you avoid the bumps in the road, then my purpose for writing it will be fulfilled. If it helps you to dust yourself off and look up after you've fallen, then I will count it as a success. More importantly, I pray that it will encourage you to trust in God's divine power and plans for your life.

Sometimes we find ourselves in dire situations and can't figure out how we got there. Sometimes circumstances are beyond our control and they alter our situation. However, most often our predicaments are the result of the choices we have made. None of us is immune to making poor decisions. (We have all bought shoes that didn't fit.) They usually seem to make perfect sense at the time but wreak pain and crisis in our lives later. When we know better, we're expected to do better. However, we all try to do the best we can with what we know, no matter how inadequate the knowledge.

Just remember, when you find yourself in a mess of your own making, you are not destined to stay there forever. May just one kernel in this book encourage you to get up, clean yourself off and keep on keeping on. I know that getting up and getting on is not always easy because I have walked in your shoes, my sister. Just keep on praying and taking one step at a time.

At times, we need to share our pains and triumphs with each other. I think we draw strength and encouragement from one another as we realize that our stories really are not as unique as we may have thought. Sharing another sister's joy and pain can be just the extra push we need to keep us hanging in just a little bit longer.

I have found comfort and inspiration in a variety of places and I joyfully share these resources with you. Sometimes I include a scripture, a book, a song or a thought I found particularly inspiring. Since my friends accuse me of knowing more songs than anybody they know, I thought it was only fitting to include the song references. It is my prayer that these words will find their way to the essence of your pain and serve as a healing balm.

Jetola Anderson-Blair

FAVORITE SCRIPTURES

I praise you for I am fearfully and wonderfully made; your works are wonderful. I know that full well. Psalms 139:14

For I know the plans I have for you, declares the Lord, plans to prosper you and not to harm you, plans to give you hope and a future. Jeremiah 29:11

Fear not, for I have redeemed you; I have summoned you by name; you are mine. When you pass through the waters, I will be with you; and when you pass through the rivers, they will not sweep over you. When you walk through the fire, you will not be burned; the flames will not set you ablaze. Isaiah 43: 1-2

I am my sister and my sister is me. We have celebrated each other's joys and cried each other's tears. We have walked in each other's shoes.

JEAB

TABLE OF CONTENTS

TABLE OF CONTENTS CONTINUED

THE BIRTHDAY GIFT

When we are young, we can't wait for our birthdays, especially the significant ones like sixteen (driver's license), eighteen (voter's registration), twenty-one (legal everywhere). As a matter of fact , I am sure you have noticed that children will be very specific with the fractional portion of their age or they will quote their age as being "almost" the next age. They are never plain ten; but ten and a half or "almost" eleven. However, somewhere around twenty-five the attitude changes for a lot of people and they actually become depressed when their birthdays get here.

I am often thrown for a loop when one of my friends is unhappy on her birthday and sees it as a cause to be depressed. I can't even relate to that! I have fully accepted that each birthday is a gift from God and that I did nothing to deserve it so, the least I can do is be grateful. I also feel very liberated by the process of growing older because I am more in tune with my feelings and other people's opinion of me matter less each year.

One area of my life where I feel especially liberated is in my friendships. These days, I speak my truth clearly and honestly in my friendships and I take ownership of my feelings. If you hurt my feelings, I will tell you so, instead of pouting about it and holding a grudge. This comes with age. At twenty-five I could not have made such a claim because I didn't want to hurt anyone's feelings. In the name of sparing others, I would hurt myself instead.

In retrospect, I realize that I have kept many a friendship going long past its last gasp because I either failed to see or chose not to see the one-sided nature of the relationship. It never mattered to me that I was the one to always remember birthdays, anniversaries, and every other special event and there was little reciprocation. It never mattered to me that the last time we spoke I made the phone call, and the time before that, and the time before that as well.

My grandmother used to say that if you want to know who's rowing the boat, you need to drop your oar. One year I decided to take that advice to heart and apply it as an experiment. At the beginning of the year I made my usual round of phone calls and mailed out cards and notes. On the surface everything was just fine; everyone was happy to hear from me and wouldn't get off the phone. This time it would all be different, though, because I consciously decided that I wasn't initiating any more phone calls and wouldn't be sending any notes after my birthday. In other words, I was ready to take on a new attitude to go with my new age. I was going to rest my oars and see what would happen to the boat.

Not surprisingly, there were very few phone calls forthcoming and, as I wasn't making any, Southwestern Bell and Sprint probably went into shock when my phone bills fell to the bare minimum. The boat just stood still and would not move in any direction. At first, it was a little painful but eventually the pain passed and I came to realize that I had given all I could to these friendships and there was nothing coming back. Therefore, I wasn't really losing anything. (Getting older can clarify your perspective like that!)

Now my Christmas and birthday lists are shorter than they have ever been, but the friendships I have are far more meaningful. Now instead of a long line of one-sided relationships, I have a short list of friends I can call at 2:00 o'clock in the morning with any crisis and they will say, "Tell me what you need me to do." To have one such person in your life who values you that much is a blessing and to have several is a miracle. I know I am enjoying a miracle because I have foregone quantity for quality and I have no regrets. I pray each day that I will continue to be the person these friends can also call at 2:00 a.m. and after I stumble around in the dark and knock things off the nightstand, my only question will be, "What do you need me to do?"

When one of my non-rowing friend's birthday or other special occasion comes up, I don't forget; I send up a special wish for her from wherever I am but I no longer feel the need or compulsion to run out and buy a card/gift or make a phone call. To me, that's the liberation borne of age. Now you see why I like this getting older thing!

One day I was at the tennis court watching two friends hitting balls and that observation also helped to clarify the situation for me even more. Specifically, one had a bucket of balls that she would throw to the other and the hitter would return them hitting them all over the place, but never back to her. Eventually, the bucket became empty and the hitter climbed over the net and they recovered the balls and refilled the bucket. I smiled because I realized that what had happened with these friendships was that my bucket became empty because I just kept tossing my balls across the net and they were never coming back.

If you have had a similar experience and guilt is keeping you from moving on even though you are getting nothing out of the relationship, release yourself from the guilt and just walk away. It will hurt at first and feel weird for a long time, but, eventually, you will feel very liberated by the experience and you will grow personally. A relationship that's only kept alive by means of artificial respiration will only deplete resources. It will never contribute anything useful to one's growth.

The ability to open your eyes and see things clearly and be honest about what you see is the ultimate birthday gift. Shakespeare admonished us to be true to ourselves above all things. However, truth is the offspring of wisdom and wisdom is the fruit of age. The bottom line is that aging gives us the gift of clarity and with clarity we can make better choices in all areas of our lives. However, if we overlook or undervalue this gift, we are cheating ourselves and stunting our growth, thereby becoming our own worst enemy.

SONG:
ConFunkShun: I'm Leaving You For Me.

THOUGHT:
Sometimes it's better to pull the plug.

SCRIPTURE:
This is the day the Lord has made; let us rejoice and be glad in it.
Psalm 118:24

WATERFORD CRYSTAL OR JELLY JAR?

I have lived in many places and each move required adjusting to cultural differences and fitting in with local ways. Yet, I have found that no matter where I live, I am a New Yorker to the core. A big part of the New York identity comes from having experienced the joy of shopping in the two vastly different worlds of Bloomingdale's and Job Lot.

No matter how good a deal you get in your high-end store, there are just some things that you buy at Woolworth's, Job Lot and the flea market. Have you ever noticed how you act differently in each store? One atmosphere demands dignified behavior and one allows you to just let it all hang out. This phenomenon has always fascinated me because it also pops up in different ways in our life experiences. One area in particular where it is especially evident is the love arena.

Have you ever noticed how some women are treated with respect regardless of who the man is while other women are treated so badly that one is tempted to look for the "treat me like dirt" sign? For example, there are some women to whom a man will apologize to the skies, if he so much as says "damn" around them and there are some women that men treat like locker buddies. The most fascinating thing is when the same man dogs out one woman and treats another like she is the Queen of Sheba. I don't know about you but I can't help but wonder why. How did he know how to treat them? Where did he get the script?

My pastor once preached a sermon targeted to the men of

7

the church in which he admonished them to treat their wives like Waterford crystal instead of like jelly jars. That sermon got me thinking about the role we, as women, play in the way we are treated. The truth of the matter is that the way others treat us is a function of how we treat ourselves. If we treat ourselves like a flea market with stuff scattered on the floor, others will have no inclination to pick up and carefully put back anything that falls out of place. Instead, they will just pile more junk onto what already exists.

On the other hand, if something about you says "this sister is not to be trifled with", the likelihood that someone is going to come along and treat you like a jelly jar and get away with it is greatly decreased. I am sure you have noticed that in the stores the fine jewelry is locked away and the cheap costume stuff is left out for everybody to handle as they please. There is a lesson to be learned in that simple marketing technique—merchandise of value is treated with respect.

Every now and again we need to stop and take inventory of ourselves and our behaviors to see what message they send to the world around us. Do men say "excuse me" when they say "damn" in your presence or do they treat you like a locker room buddy? Are you generally treated with respect and high regard? Ask yourself why or why not. How you are treated is up to you--bargain basement sale or high-class store? Jelly jar or fine crystal? The answer is up to you.

SONG: Aretha Franklin: Respect

READING: Maya Angelou: Phenomenal Woman

8

THOSE SHOES LOOK GOOD, BUT THEY SURE DO HURT

I own a pair of bronze designer pumps that are just a beautiful sight to behold. Every time I wear them, I get compliments from men and women alike. I bought those shoes because they were gorgeous and the price was right. Besides, my girlfriend convinced me I couldn't live without them. The truth be told, though, they did not fit right in the store and have never been comfortable since the day I bought them, but I convinced myself with the old "they will stretch" argument. I know just about every sister reading this can relate to the gorgeous pair of shoes that looks great but hurts so bad that you see stars. Nevertheless, we ignore the pain and twist our feet, curl our toes, push on the shoehorn and do whatever we have to do to force ourselves into them.

I think the shoe thing is symbolic of some of the other crazy stuff we do in our lives. It represents the uncomfortable situations we stay in long past the time we should have left. How many times have we stayed in relationships that drained our energy, our finances and our emotions, while getting nothing in return and made excuses for staying? I am sure you know the excuses...he's fine; he has a job; he has a nice car; being with him beats being alone, at least I got a man and so on and so on. How many times have we stayed in jobs we hated to the point where they were making us physically ill because they paid the bills and maintained our lifestyles? How many times have we stayed because we didn't want to have to start over somewhere else or we just knew we wouldn't be able to find a comparable job (without even looking)? How many times have we said "yes"

9

when we wanted to say "no", then lived with resentment? Don't beat up yourself. We have all done it but there comes a time when you must speak up.

I consider my grandmother to be one of the wisest souls that ever lived and she never gave complicated advice. On more occasions that I can count, I have heard her say, "If it don't fit, don't force it or you'll break it." Somehow, as we grow older, we don't seem to listen as well and we end up missing many of the messages which could help us avoid pain. But that same simple advice that my grandmother gave me years ago still applies in numerous situations. Thankfully, most of us are still somewhat in touch with the small voice that whispers in our ears to warn us of danger. Unfortunately, we often ignore it and force ourselves into shoes that don't fit, then suffer the pain.

When we force ourselves into shoes that don't fit well, we may put on an intact front for the world but we can't deny the pain to ourselves. There is comfort in the familiar, and change, in general, and the unknown, in particular, can be disconcerting. However, when there's that little voice telling you that you deserve better than you are getting from a relationship, when you lay in bed at night thinking about calling in sick so that you don't have to go to that job you hate, when you really are sick because of that job you hate, it is time to abandon the comfort of the familiar, take off those tight shoes, and let your feet breathe. Your body and spirit will thank you.

Only you know what your "bronze shoe" is and only you can take it off. All the advice from your friends and family will not make you change a thing. However, when you no longer have time for the pain (mentally, emotionally, psychologically and physically), you will do what you need to do. I think one of the most frustrating life experiences is having others tell us the solutions to our problems before we are ready to solve them. Talking about what's wrong in our lives and being ready to make a change are two very different situations. Sometimes we shop around for the answer we want to hear and reject all others that don't fit our preconceived notions. Doing this simply wastes the time of both you and your advisors. The answers you seek are already in you, but you will only recognize them when you are ready.

FOOD FOR THOUGHT:
I don't have to wear tight shoes.

SONG:
Carly Simon: Haven't Got Time For The Pain

SCRIPTURE:
God has not deserted us in our bondage. Ezra 9:9

Jetola E. Anderson-Blair

SLOT MACHINE LOVE

I will say this about myself straight up front: I do not like to lose, especially not my hard-earned money. That character trait is so deep that it greatly affects all aspects of my life. Several years ago, I was on assignment in Puerto Rico and for several weeks I stayed at a fancy hotel with its own casino. For some people this would be a good thing or a bad thing, but for me it was an indifferent thing because I knew I was neither in danger of getting rich (after all I wouldn't have known what to do with myself) or going broke (in the stores perhaps but definitely not in the casino).

Even though I didn't gamble, I loved hanging out in the casino people watching. I was always fascinated by the look the gamblers got in their eyes when they told themselves, "The next one is the big one." While I enjoyed watching all the gamblers, the slot machine players were my favorite. I would watch them feed the machines coin after coin and every so often they would win back a few coins. I suppose the occasional win was essential to the lure of the promise that "the next one could be the big one" and it was surely effective in keeping them seated and feeding the machine.

Watching these people pour their money into the slot machines put me in one of my retrospective moods. First I thought about all the shoes I could buy with the money they were throwing away. Next I started thinking about how we often squander ourselves on relationships which give nothing in return because we hope that one day he will change into our dream man. I am not sure if it is a genetic or environmental trait

12

but women certainly know how to make excuses for situations that don't sit right.

I think it is important to establish some personal standards and determine what our needs are from a relationship before we even become involved. This way, when someone comes along, we have a yardstick by which to measure how the relationship meets our needs. We rarely ever do this because we are taught to be the caregivers and nurturers. True to form, we give and give in relationships (this is a good thing when it's is a two-way street, but not so when it is all one-sided) and often get little or nothing in return. For many of us, the response to not getting our needs met is to give even more. Yes, we just pump our love, energy, dreams, money, etc. into the slot machine with the constant hope that the next one will be "the big one."

Instead of acknowledging that the other party is coming up short, we often put the blame on ourselves...he's so busy with work and I shouldn't be so needy; my birthday isn't a big deal; I don't need a card, a gift or flowers. This is where your list comes in handy as a reality check. You can ask yourself or a friend, "Am I too demanding?" "Do I expect too much?" If you answer those questions realistically, and the answer is that your needs are reasonable but unmet, then you need to ask yourself the more pressing question "is this relationship a slot machine?"

When you come up with a conclusive answer to the question, it is important to make some decisions and take some action. Whining and complaining about the situation will be useless, if you are unprepared to do something about it. Eventually, your loved ones will get tired of your moaning and groaning and they will no longer be sympathetic to your slot machine losses.

FOOD FOR THOUGHT:
There is a time to stay and a time to leave.

SONG:
Vanessa Rubin: Arise and Shine

SCRIPTURE:
There is a time for everything and a season for every activity under heaven…a time to search and a time to give up, a time to keep and a time to throw away. Ecclesiastes 3:1,6

For I am fearfully and wonderfully made. Your works are wonderful, I know that full well. Psalms 139:14

Do not give dogs what is sacred; do not throw your pearls to pigs. Matthew 7:6

WHERE DOES THE TIME GO?

Sometimes I am convinced that I have split personalities when it comes to managing my time. If I have something to do which I enjoy, I will run out and take care of the details way in advance. For example, my summer vacation plans are typically nailed down by the end of January. In college, if I had to write a paper on a topic of my own choosing or personal interest, I would start my research right after the class where the assignment was handed out. However, when I have some unpleasant or undesirable task to attend to, I will procrastinate until the last possible minute then run around on adrenaline.

Putting off things I had to do but didn't want to do was adding immeasurable stress to my life and manifesting itself in many ways...I was tired and irritable and unmotivated...and it was all self-inflicted. There just never seemed to be enough time to fulfill all my obligations. I had to 'come clean' and 'get straight' as the kids say. In the process I learned several significant lessons, such as, it is OK to say "no" and I really have more time than I realize.

Basketball is one of my great passions and there is nothing I love more than a well-played game with tight scores. I am constantly amazed at what two teams will accomplish with less than two minutes left on the clock in the fourth quarter. Sometimes I am forced to ask myself if the NBA has a different measure of time than the average Joe out in the street. Is a second really a second? I can't help but wonder, but I also know the truth...the time is the same and we can accomplish whatever we set our minds to do.

During the tithe and offering segment of some church services the pastor often encourages the congregation to flip through their checkbook records to see where their money goes. They often say, "Where your money is, there your heart lies also." Sometimes we need to take this same kind of inventory with our time; i.e., track for some period what we spend our time doing. Therein lies the answer to why we can't find the time to do the things that we need or want to do. One of the best lessons I learned in a time management seminar (believe me I have been to plenty) is that not everything that is important is urgent and not everything that is urgent is important. This distinction is critical in helping us determine where to spend our time.

It is a lesson I have learned well but don't always apply with diligence. I usually start out on the straight and narrow but often backslide. However, I stopped beating up on myself long ago for how I spend my time. My time is no longer directed by some external dictum, but by what is important to me. Therefore, if I want to spend a Saturday morning watching old Tina Turner concerts, I no longer feel overcome by guilt that I am not out moving mountains and setting the world on fire. Maybe a dose of Proud Mary is just what I need at that time in order to energize my body and spirit to accomplish more lofty and meaningful endeavors.

When all is said and done, we are all given the same twenty four hours each day and each second is just as long as an NBA second. However, for most of us there is more on our "To Do" plates than we could say grace over and we feel overwhelmed. My Sister, let's face it, you probably won't get it all done, but you may kill yourself trying. That does not have to be the case, though, because you have more control over the situation than you think.

Start out by asking yourself what will happen if you don't do a task. Next ask yourself how important this will be ten years from now. Also ask yourself if there is someone else who would actually enjoy this task which you dread and could you make a tradeoff. When you filter your list through this prism, you will find that many of the obligations you allow to drive you crazy can actually be eliminated or delegated, thus freeing up your time to attend to the things which are truly important to you.

I think the saddest epitaph which could ever be written about anyone is "Here lies ____. She did all the things she should have but never had time to do the things she wanted to." If we allow our lives to be dictated by the "shoulds" of others, we will forever stifle our authentic selves and our dreams will wither on their vines.

It is neither practical nor realistic to think we can blow off everything in our lives to concentrate on what we want. However, every second that we reclaim for ourselves and apply to something meaningful to us empowers us to fulfill our dreams. Remember the "one day" list you have been compiling in the back of your mind? One day I am going to do this and one day I am going to do that. Bear in mind that "one day" never comes but the accumulation of seconds, minutes and hours will lead you to your starting point that will create your "one day."

If something is on your "one day" list, it got there for a reason. Most likely, the reason is that it will bring you some element of enjoyment, satisfaction or a sense of accomplishment. No matter what your circumstances are, no one is depriving you from tackling that "one day" list. You are in control and when you are ready, you'll find the time. "One day" can only come when you make time for it.

It's up to you to decide how important that dream list is and how willing you are to tackle it. You can choose to make excuses and watch time pass you by or you can say "Today is the day." Your choice will either leave you to regret or rejoice. Choose wisely, my sister.

FOOD FOR THOUGHT: There is enough time.

SONG:
Patti LaBelle: There's a Winner in You

BOOKS:
Stephen Covey: First Things First
                 The Seven Habits of Highly Effective People

IT IS ALWAYS TOO SOON TO QUIT

The first time I heard Herbie Hancock play the piano, I thought to myself "I want to play like that." The idea isn't so far-fetched except for the fact that I quit piano lessons at fourteen because I couldn't stand to practice. Whenever we observe an expert performing a task, we think we can do as well and sometimes we are actually inspired to take lessons or make whatever baby steps are required to get us on our way. In my own case, I am easily frustrated because the amateur version always seems so inadequate when compared to the expert. Instead of putting in the effort to build up to the next level, I think about quitting.

Thankfully, I have often had someone there to talk me out of quitting or my guilty conscience overcame me with echoes of the rhyme from my childhood "Winners never quit and quitters never win." We live in frustrating times and sometimes quitting is the easy way out, but we have to keep our minds focused on whatever the goal is that we have set for ourselves. Also, there are people who, because of their own agendas, would love to see us give up our dreams. If you spend enough time around them, they will talk you out of your goal. They will tell you that you are too old, too short, too fat, too skinny, too light, too black, too whatever to accomplish your goal. It is critical to stay away from these dream stealers. If you allow them, they will poison your dreams and cause them to die without ever seeing the light of day.

I recently read a story about a woman who started medical

19

school in her forties and I remember thinking 'that takes guts.' I am sure she had all the naysayers with their lists of reasons not to do it. I am sure it has not been easy but, deep inside, she must feel so proud of herself. A dream is an essential part of living because, without one, we're just existing, no different from any other living creature on the planet Earth. However, when we come up against obstacles, quitting sometimes seems like an attractive option. If we just hang in there a little longer, whatever the situation may be, success may be just around the corner.

It is always too soon to quit because if we were doing a crossword puzzle, quit would be a four-letter word for regret. When we quit, we relegate ourselves to living the rest of our lives wondering about what might have been. That's a heavy burden to bear and it affects us in ways we don't even begin to realize. George Washington Carver probably tried hundreds of experiments before he came up with peanut butter. If he had quit at the one just before, just think how lonely jelly would have been and how parents would have had to find some other comfort food when little Johnny starts to whine.

When you are pursuing a dream, it is a given that there will be obstacles set in your way to test your patience and your resilience. Success comes from recognizing the obstacles as challenges and recognizing the role they play in getting you closer to your dream. If you find a way around them, you are that much closer. If you regard them as insurmountable, they will stop you in your tracks and make you retreat and quit one moment before you strike success.

When the option of quitting begins to appear more attractive than all other alternatives, just remember the song from The Preacher's Wife "Help is on the Way." It is always too soon to quit and we usually quit because we are relying on our own strength. When we recognize the need to go to a power that is higher than we are and tap into that source of strength, we will hang on just a little bit longer and that extra step may be just what it takes to make it to our dream. We will remember Isaiah 20:49 which promises that He gives strength to the weary and increases the power of the weak.

SONG: Jimmy Cliff: You Can Get It If You Really Want

BOOKS: Les Brown: It's Not Over Until You Win!
                     Les Brown: Live Your Dreams

SOMETIMES YOU MUST BELIEVE BEFORE YOU CAN SEE

Our society does not place much faith in the things unseen. As a matter of fact, the average person most likely adheres to the philosophy "seeing is believing." I am here to suggest that sometimes you must believe before you can see. If believing is restricted to only that which can be seen, the range of life's possibilities will be reduced to a mere fraction.

As Black women, we do not hear a lot of positive reinforcing messages from the media. By the sins of omission or commission, we are fed negative messages about ourselves every day. Eventually, these messages will take a toll on our psyche and lead us to believe we are not beautiful or smart. Subliminally, we are told that the extent of what we have to offer society is the hoochi-coochi mama running around half-naked in the music videos or the expert on household cleaning products whose measure of worth is determined by the cleanliness of her house. The other option is the neck-twisting-palm-raising talk show princess trying to identify her "baby daddy." We know in our hearts that we are so much more than these images represent. Yet, if that is all we see, it is all we will believe.

As members of "the village", we are charged with lifting each other up and believing positive thoughts about ourselves and the Sisterhood. Since the messages around us attempt to negate our being at every turn, it's easy to believe what we hear about ourselves everyday. However, if we instinctively believe in each other's goodness as well as our own, we will start to treat each other as if we believe we are bright, beautiful, compassionate, etc. The end result will be a self-fulfilling prophecy because we will start to respond to the way we treat ourselves and the positive traits will be in evidence for all the world to see.

Believing in the existence of inherent goodness in each person will not create it if it's not already there, but denying its existence will drive it into remission. When the media and the other messages around us fail to validate us, we need to turn to ourselves in the mirror and in each other and reinforce all that's positive. By believing in the positive and affirming and claiming it, we will begin to see it.

Sometimes our vision is clouded by all the negative messages we receive about ourselves and we are only able to see ourselves as others see us, usually in a negative way. We owe it to ourselves and to each other to look beyond the negative images and tune into the true self which was created in the image of greatness. Do you remember how the old black and white TVs would get two channels mixed up and you had to slowly turn the tuning dial until one picture would fade away and the other picture emerged clearly? We are dealing with the same thing where our true selves are concerned and we have to keep turning that tuning button in order to block out all the negative and bring the richness and beauty of ourselves into clear focus.

SONGS: Jimmy Cliff: I Can See Clearly Now
              R. Kelly: I Believe I Can Fly

OLD WOUNDS WON'T HEAL IF YOU KEEP PICKING THE SCABS

As a child, I loved to pick the scabs off my battle wounds---skinned knees, scratches, scrapes, etc. The adults in my life would say "Stop picking; it won't heal." As an adult, I have noticed that sometimes we still pick at our battle wounds instead of letting them heal. Sometimes we just can't move forward because the old wounds are still open and the pain keeps us immobilized and clinging to the past.

Letting go is not easy because holding on is familiar -- kind of like an old bathrobe. However, letting go is the source of healing and growth. When true healing has transpired, the scar may occasionally remind us of the pain but we no longer feel it. The act of releasing old pains and grudges frees us up to enjoy the here and now and what it offers. Forgiving ourselves and others has the power to salve the deepest pain and detonate the most powerful heartache.

Let's face it. All our parents, friends and relatives probably did something we wished they hadn't done or didn't do something we think they should have. Maybe you were right to feel angry or betrayed when the incident occurred, but if you keep holding on to it forever, you will never get past it. There has to be a statute of limitation on parental crimes, real and imagined. I don't say any of this flippantly or as if I think it's easy. I have been guilty of holding on to anger and grudges so long that I have sometimes forgotten what the source of those feeling was. Eventually, one day I just got up and said, "This doesn't make any sense," and initiated contact with the person and extended a gesture of peace.

I am not suggesting that your gesture will automatically result in smooth sailing and perfect reconciliation. Sometimes reconciliation is not possible, but the act of forgiveness puts you in a different place spiritually. Also, sometimes reconciliation is not the answer. The issue here is forgiving and letting go, not necessarily kissing and making up. The truth is that some people do not need to be in your life and you are better off loving them from afar and keeping them in your prayers. As long as you have established forgiveness in your heart, communicated it and let the matter go, your scabs will heal and fall off. It is the act of holding on which causes festering and impedes healing.

So far, I have talked about forgiveness and letting go as they relate to others, but sometimes the person we need to forgive most is ourselves. Our lives are the sum total of the choices we have made and we have all made bad choices along the way. Sometimes we linger in regret about choices we made or didn't make for years after the decision. For some reason, it seems that we are harder on ourselves than we would be on anyone else or than anyone else would ever be on us. We criticize and hold on to "woulda's", "coulda's", "shoulda's" and "what if's" way past their usefulness. Yes, it is imperative that we learn from our mistakes or we are destined to repeat them. However, at some point, we need to say "I messed up; I can't change the past; I have to get over it," and get on with our lives. Picking at the old scabs only holds us back and prolongs the pain. The greatest gift you can give yourself is to forgive yourself and others.

There is a certain freedom and a lightness of being that only come with letting go. I have noticed when I am traveling and carrying a small bag, it becomes heavier and heavier, the longer I carry it. The same is true with our psychological and emotional baggage. No matter how light they are when we start out, they will become increasingly heavier and weight us down the longer we hold on to them. If we are weighed down and tired, we will not be able to appreciate the soul-stirring joy when it comes our way.

SONGS:

Anita Baker:	No More Tears
Daryl Coley:	He's Already Forgiven

SCRIPTURE:

I have loved you with an everlasting love; I have drawn you with loving kindness. Jeremiah 31:3

MAYBE IT'S YOU

Sometimes we find ourselves in relationships which just work our last good nerve and no matter what we do, our interaction with the other person is just stressful and unpleasant. This person could be a boss, spouse, parent, coworker, sibling or child. Sometimes we get in the other person's face, sometimes we avoid them and sometimes we decide to take them to the cross. We'll pray, "Lord, please change this person's attitude, please set them straight, etc." Somehow it seems God doesn't hear us and things remain the same or sometimes get worse.

In these times we need to pull back and reexamine ourselves in order to help us figure out why God didn't answer our prayers and what the message is that he is sending with His silence. Oftentimes He is saying, "I am not interested in the other person; I want to deal with you first." That is a difficult message to hear because when we have convinced ourselves that the other person is the problem, we can't even entertain the idea that it could be us.

God often designs these master plans which escape our understanding but that doesn't stop us from trying to run things. After all, you know how much we love to be in charge. Clearly, when outcomes don't match our expectations or desires, we often feel the need to step in and give God a helping hand. When someone is working our nerves and it is all their fault, we want to make sure God knows despite any indications to the contrary.

While it is typically not our nature to say, "maybe it's me", sometimes that is exactly what we need to do. I know in my own case I can be very impatient and don't easily entertain what I consider to be fools or foolishness. Over the years, I have come to realize that some of my interactions which were fraught with frustration were God's way of helping me become more patient. It doesn't always work because sometimes it is still easier to point the finger at the other person.

Sometimes the other person is chronically in a bad mood, snaps at the least little thing and irritates you in every situation. Self-examination may lead you to realize that the other person is lonely, frustrated, and in need of a friend. Surely, it is easier to snap back and offer this person a few choice words, but if you can hear the small voice encouraging you to be a friend to that person in spite of his/her ways, you need to reach out and be that friend.

As is always the case, when we listen to God's word and follow His will, He smiles at us in pleasure. You will know this from the satisfaction you will get from the reduction in tension. You will learn more about the other person and yourself and realize that while it may seem otherwise, maybe the problem is you.

THOUGHT:
I will look at myself first.

SCRIPTURE:
Search me, Oh God, and know my heart. Psalm 139:23

DEAD BATTERIES DON'T LIE

For several weeks I knew that the battery in the remote control for my car alarm was running low because I had to keep moving closer and closer to the car to activate a response. One day I got to the parking lot and I couldn't get even the slightest sound from the alarm. However, I didn't panic because I knew what the problem was and I was not in a hurry.

Thankfully, one of my girlfriends walked out at the same time and the two of us jimmied the remote case with a nail file. We turned the battery around a few times and closed the case. Lo and behold, the remote started working again. I nervously drove to my next stop all the time mentally planning that I had to buy a replacement battery. However, I got busy and distracted and did not get around to it.

That dead battery played quite a trick on me, though. For several days it continued working just fine, luring me into a false sense of security until I just forgot that I needed to replace it. Another day, I got off work and hurried to the parking lot with my mind racing and prioritizing all the things I had to get done that evening. I walked up to the car and pressed the remote and was met with blasting silence. This time I still didn't panic but I was very annoyed because it was drizzling and I was in a big hurry.

As fate would have it, the same girlfriend walked out again and this time she was laughing at me. "Girl, I thought you said you were going to get a new battery last week. What happened?" My face burned with embarrassment as I sheepishly replied, "It started acting right and I forgot there was anything

29

wrong with it." We tried the jimmy trick again but this time there was no cooperation on the part of the battery and I knew I had to concede and take care of business right then and there. My friend drove me to the nearest Radio Shack to get a new battery.

The salesman tried to convince us the problem was with the remote itself and not the battery. I kept insisting it was the battery and he wanted to know how I knew. I told him, "When I jiggled it, it worked for a while then it went back to its old ways." He tested it and sure enough, it was completely dead. (Lesson learned: Trust your instincts.) Replacement in hand, we drove back to the office. I deactivated the alarm from halfway across the parking lot and, before long, I was on my merry way.

As I drove along the freeway (completely behind schedule), I couldn't help but think about what had just happened and how the lesson applied to other areas in my life. I have had people in my life reveal their true natures by disappointing me repeatedly. However, when I claimed my feelings and admitted to being hurt by their behavior or "jiggle" them some other way, they straightened up for a while and I forgot their shortcomings. Without failure, they would slip back to their old ways, usually at the most inopportune time for me. Just when I allowed myself to trust and rely on someone whom I have known to be unreliable and inconsistent in the past, they would switch back to "dead battery" mode. Amazingly, I would actually be surprised and think "but he's been acting so right lately." or "I didn't even think she was like that anymore."

I am not saying that people can't change. The world would be in a very sad state of affairs if we couldn't hold on to the hope of change both for ourselves and for those around us. However, we must remain on our guard in order to protect our feelings, our hopes and our dreams. If someone has revealed himself to be one way over the course of time but appears to have gone through a transformation because you threw a fit or had some other kind of confrontation over their behavior, you need to tread lightly. The apparent change may be in response to the jiggling on your part and not an authentic conversion. I am not encouraging perpetual distrust; I am saying it's important to stay alert and look for evidence of genuine change or you could find yourself with a "dead battery" at the time when you can least afford it.

I am heeding the lesson in my own life: I am trying not to be fooled by superficial character changes. I know that I will make mistakes in judgment along the way, but I expect the lessons to be learned from those slipups to be reinforcement for what I learned from this experience. If someone is going to be the way I want them to be just because I require it, I have to be cautious.

THOUGHT: It is up to me to heed the warning.

YOU HAVE TO KNOW WHEN TO LEAVE THE PARTY

As a child I took things very literally so I had a difficult time understanding some of my grandmother's favorite expressions. For example, she used to say, "You have to know when to leave the party." and that made no sense to me because I was never at a party when she would say it. I guess the evidence of adulthood for me is that not only do I understand the expression, I have been known to use it on occasion.

By all means, I am a strong supporter of hanging in there and giving your best shot to any situation but I also recognize the importance of knowing when to leave the party. Sometimes we stay in situations for all the wrong reasons even when all indicators tell us we should leave. We are so good at rationalizing our staying that we even start to believe the lies we tell ourselves.

I was driving to work one day and listening to Sinbad's audio book and he made the point that if a man was a lazy bum when you met him, he'll still be a lazy bum when you marry him. Sometimes we get caught up in the fantasy of thinking we can change the situation. As a result, we hang in there and we give more than one hundred percent in an effort to make the relationship work. However, despite all our efforts, the person hasn't changed and sometimes the shortcomings become even more pronounced.

We sometimes cling to external reasons for staying in situations that are clearly wrong for us. For example: "There has never been a divorce in my family so I am not going to be the first."; "My parents got divorced and I am going to make my marriage last no matter what."; "My snobbish sister got divorced and I want to prove that I can do one thing better than her."; "What will people think of me?"; "I don't want to be a failure so I can't leave." and so on and so on. Sometimes our families and friends are the ones pushing us to stay, even though we know in our hearts that we need to burn rubber and be on our way.

MEN

If you are with a man who doesn't have any room in his life for God, you'd better know when to leave the party.

If you are living with a man who can't make it home with his paycheck Friday night because he blows every last dime at the local betting shop or icehouse, you'd better know when to leave the party.

If you are marriage minded and have been dating a man for years and every time you bring up the topic of marriage he breaks out into a sweat and starts to stammer, you'd better know when to leave the party.

If you are with a man who has proven that he is unable or unwilling to be faithful, you'd better know when to leave the party.

33

If you are with a man who refuses to find honest work, you'd better know when to leave the party.

If you're with a man who has no interest in personal growth and is still talking about the same old tired stuff from 15 years ago, you'd better know when to leave the party.

If you are with a man who consistently makes promises and breaks them, you better know when to leave the party.

If you are with a man who puts you down and makes you feel like dirt about yourself, you better know when to leave the party.

If you are with a man who treats your feelings like they don't matter and doesn't even get it when you complain, you better know when to leave the party.

WORK

If you are fine all weekend long but you get a killer headache or stomachache every Sunday night as soon as you think about going back to work, you'd better know when to leave the party.

If you are bored out of your mind and can feel your mind turning to mushy oatmeal, you'd better know when to leave the party.

If your skills and talents are being completely underutilized and you are not learning anything new, you'd better know when to leave the party.

If you spend the majority of your at work time wishing you were somewhere else, you'd better know when to leave the party.

If you can't stand anyone at your job and the feeling is mutual, you'd better know when to leave the party.

If nothing you do is ever right in your supervisor's eyes and you are playing hostess to a lot of uncharitable thoughts about him or her, you'd better know when to leave the party.

If the best part of your job is having lunch with your friends, you'd better know when to leave the party.

If the job brings you no satisfaction beyond paying the bills, you'd better know when to leave the party.

We can always find reasons for staying when we should leave, but it takes real courage to get up and leave especially when we are uncertain of what awaits us on the outside. The unknown is scary but chances are it's not as bad as the known. God did not mean for us to be unhappy and if we are, we need to do something about it. Above all, don't complain about what's wrong with the man or the job or whatever and then do nothing about it. That gets very tired really fast and no one will want to hear about it.

THE PROBLEM WITH POTENTIAL

I once met a delightful woman at a vendors' fair. She was charmed by my accent and, before long, we were engaged in a long conversation which touched on a variety of subjects. When I told her I was from Jamaica, she wanted my advice about Jamaican men. I told her I couldn't offer her any advice on Jamaican men because I could only speak of the one I was dating. (I have since married him.) She then shared with me that she was dating a nice Jamaican man who was not quite what she wanted but he had so much potential. Those words made me cringe and shiver because I have never known of a situation where falling in love with someone's potential yielded happy results.

That conversation brought back to mind one of my dear grandmother's sayings, "God sees us as we could be but he loves us as we are." I told that sister if she was not satisfied with what he is today and was banking on his potential, she was writing a prescription for disappointment. I know I have strong opinions about many issues but this is a road I have definitely walked and can speak about from experience. I remember being very much in love with a man who was not quite what I wanted him to be, but I convinced myself that if I loved him enough, he could become the person I knew he could be. Big mistake!! If only I knew then what I know now, I would have saved myself a lot of time, money, emotions, energy and pain. Unfortunately, we often learn best from our own mistakes and I was an A student.

The problem with someone else's potential is that it is

usually our creation or vision and often has nothing to do with who the person is or desires to be. We do not have the power or the skills to truly change someone. Even if they go through the motions in order to appease us, the change will not be genuine and eventually the authentic self will manifest itself. We then have a menu of emotions to select from -- anger, pain, disappointment, resentment, etc. Who do we blame as we are eating from this buffet?

It's easy to point the finger at the other person and focus on how he let us down, but if we are honest with ourselves, we will realize that we lifted him to an unnatural height and he returned to his comfort zone. Think of the times when you relaxed your hair bone-straight but, given the right combination of heat and humidity, it would revert to its natural state, as if it had never met a bottle of relaxer. It's the same thing. All you need are the right circumstances.

I once heard a pastor tell the story of a woman who said as long as the man can conjugate a verb she can fix him. Another pastor spoke of another woman whose standard in mate selection was simply the ability to match his socks. If that's all you require, there's nothing wrong with that but don't pretend that's enough when deep in your heart you know you want all these other qualities. A person isn't a broken-down toaster you pick up at a garage sale with the intention of fixing it up. If you see the brother as he could be but you can't love him as he is, you need to walk on by. If only I had had the sense to do this in the past, I would have spared myself a whole lot of suffering.

It is true that some people have ridiculously long lists and are on a quest for perfection in the other person. My philosophy is that I don't need Mr. Perfect, just Mr. Perfect For Me. That is to say, I expect him to have faults but only faults with which I can live. I know what I can and can't tolerate and if someone has faults I can't tolerate, I think the fairest approach for all concerned is to let him be for someone else. For example, I consider fidelity to be a primary requirement in a relationship, yet there are some women who say "I don't care what he does as long as he doesn't do it in my face." Clearly, one of those sisters would be perfectly content with the Mr. Oh So Fine or Mr. Has the Right Job who doesn't know the meaning of the word faithful while he and I would have serious problems. But hey, one woman's junk is another woman's treasure. I do not have the skills or the desire to fix anyone up. Life is short and I figure I should be putting the effort into fixing up my own self into being the best possible me, instead of trying to rearrange someone else.

I guess it makes us feel better when we do stupid things and realize that someone has done even worse. Imagine a woman who desperately wanted children. All her life, raising a family has been her biggest dream. Nevertheless, she dated and married a man who said he didn't want children. Despite what he told her, she decided that he would make beautiful babies and he would be a great father once he saw their child and the paternal gene was activated. Wrong!! She gave birth to a special needs child and they divorced before long. Now she divides her time between raising the child as a single mother and dwelling on how her husband let her down. Nothing anyone can say to her can make her see the situation any differently.

Potential only has meaning when it is the individual's honest desire for himself and he's taking real steps towards making it a reality. If both pieces of that equation do not fall into place, the potential will never be fulfilled and somebody is going to be unhappy. That somebody doesn't have to be you and I surely don't want it to be me. Having been down that road before, if I don't heed the lessons I've learned, I deserve to be hurt. I thank God that experience is a good teacher and I am a good student. For your sake, pray that you are too.

SONG:
Barry White: Just The Way You Are

THE MAIN THING IS THE MAIN THING AND THAT'S THE MAIN THING

Sometimes the simplest expressions belie the deepest thought. I first heard the above expression shortly after I moved to Texas and I remember thinking "Oh, that's so country." Interestingly enough though, I have found that the times when I am the most confused and unfocused are also the times when I have ceased letting the main thing be the main thing. Quite frankly, I think we live in an over-stimulated society and we try to do too much. As a result, we end up losing focus and probably being less effective than we could be.

Some days I look in my planner and I am overwhelmed by all the commitments on the to-do list. I would drive myself crazy thinking that I had to do everything and do it as quickly and perfectly as possible. I was simply setting myself up for failure and major stress. I always knew I had crossed the line when my face started to hurt from clenching my teeth. When I calmed myself down and took inventory of everything I had going on, it usually turned out that I had lost track of the main thing and I was trying to make everything equally important. My grandmother used to say, "You can't line up your priorities side by side; you have to stack them." Oh, that was probably one of my least favorite expressions because the truth of it would just hit me between the eyes and the answers would be so clear. I didn't like that.

Regardless of our life situation, everyone of us will find ourselves being pulled in multiple directions at some point.

When we concentrate on the little picture, everything becomes equally important, if not critical, and we tend to react accordingly. The problem, for me, with this approach is that, before long, I feel like I have disappeared because I have given and given until there is nothing left of me. Soon I start feeling irritable and inadequate because I can't live up to all that is expected of me. When I am hopelessly unfocused and don't know the main thing from a chicken wing, I am of the least use to myself or anyone else. Those are the times I have to check myself, stack my priorities, and decide what doesn't have to get done.

I think one of my best character traits, which is also my worst flaw, is the notion that once I am committed, I think I am not allowed to change my mind. This has been a major self-improvement area for me. (See "You Have to Know When to Leave the Party.") I know that it's one of those childhood rules (like eat everything on your plate) and I can't let my adult life be dictated by every rule from my childhood. Of course, some rules are forever but I am coming to realize that this is not one of them. As a responsible and accountable adult, I have to decide where to focus my energies and what to eliminate from my pile. Unfortunately, this is much easier said than done because I am so hard on myself. Thankfully, with practice, it is getting easier.

It turns out that the simple truths really are the best because they are free from confusion. Sifting the fluff from the "stuff" allows us to accomplish more meaningful tasks and gives us a greater sense of well-being and stability. If we line up our priorities side by side, we'll never know where to start. However, when we stack them, all we have to do is start at the top. When all is said and done, the main thing is the main thing and that's the main thing. I can't believe I just said that but hey, we live and we learn. Then again, maybe I'm just country.

BOOKS:

Stephen Covey: First Things First
Richard Winwood: Time Management

SCRIPTURE:

There is a time for everything. Ecclesiastes 3:1

LIVE IN THE MOMENT

We had been experiencing Texas weather at its worst for an entire week---it was rainy, hot and humid. Try to imagine a more awful combination if you can. As for me, any day I expected to raise my arms and find mildew growing under them. Just when we were convinced we couldn't last another day, Mother Nature decided to give us a reprieve in the form of a dry, cloudless, sunny 75° morning.

As I got out of my car, I was overjoyed by the beauty of the morning. My soul woke up and I felt like I was sitting on top of a rainbow. As I walked across the parking lot, I ran into one of my coworkers and expressed my delight at the beauty of the morning. She rolled her eyes and grunted something unintelligible. I stared at her in surprise asking, "Girl, what's the matter with you?" She started by going over a laundry list of things she had to do that evening and the next day and eased into another bunch of complaints. I recoiled as if she had slapped me. Finally, I said to her, "Girl, you can't do any of that stuff now and when the time comes for you to do them, they'll be waiting for you. Just enjoy this moment; stop all that and start breathing." She insisted she didn't have time for all that cheery, cheery stuff. In that moment, I realized that we were at two different places and I made a conscious decision that I wouldn't "go there" with her. At the same time, I felt sad for her because she was allowing some other moment to ruin this particular one--the first glimpse of the sun in seven days.

This scene repeats itself in numerous variations. Recently, I was on the buffet line at a wedding reception and started making small talk with the woman ahead of me. I commented on how spectacular the whole affair had been. The ceremony had been beautiful and the facility was breathtaking. She half-heartedly shared my enthusiasm for all that was going on around us then started to complain that Monday was almost here and she would have to go back to work---this was 7:30 Saturday evening!

I told her Monday was a day and a half away and had nothing to do with that moment. She admitted that I had a point but she wasn't looking forward to going back to work. (I didn't even bother with my "you should be grateful you have a job" speech). I kept telling her to tune out the voice that kept bringing in Monday and focus on now. Eventually we went through the line and returned to our tables. I am not sure if she was really convinced to change her view but I know that I tried.

I wish I could say I always follow my own advice but I can't. I have my guilty moments when I will start thinking about stuff that happened in the past and allow "woulda", "coulda" and "shoulda" and "if only" to take over my now. Sometimes my mind races ahead in time and the present is suffocated by "what if" and her sisters.

Thankfully, I am more conscious these days and I usually catch myself early in the process and say "stop it." I am sure there are people who think I am a little touched but this technique keeps me sane and in the moment. I still slip up more often than I would like but the awareness is powerful. My mantra is "Live in the moment; it's new and special and it's just for you; once it's gone, it's gone for good and there will be not another like it." It keeps me on track most of the time.

Ask yourself how you give up your moments and try to reclaim them by blocking out the voices that drag you back to the past or push you into the future, robbing you of this moment. Find your own mantra and live in the moment.

SONGS:

Joe Cocker:	Up Where We Belong
Whitney Houston:	One Moment in Time
Bob Marley:	Three Little Birds

SCRIPTURE:

Who of you by worrying can add a single hour to his life?
Matthew 6:27

WHO'S DRIVING YOUR LIFE?

Recently, two friends and I were going to visit another friend who lived about thirty miles away. Although I was driving, only the friend in the back seat knew how to get to our destination. She gave very good directions...turn left at the next light, turn right at the gas station, etc. Based on her good directions, we eventually pulled into the driveway at our friend's house. The fact that we arrived at our destination based on the back seat instructions had a very strong impact on me.

Yes I was in the driver's seat but I was merely following instructions and not exercising free will or choice. How often do we do the same thing in our lives where we give up control to someone else and find ourselves living their dreams? If we look back at ourselves 10 - 15 years ago and identify the goals and visions we held for ourselves then and realize that today we are completely off course, we must ask ourselves "why?" Could it be that we started taking back seat instructions, ignored our own counsel and instincts and lost our way? It happens all the time and sometimes the drift is so subtle that we don't notice it. We simply wake up one day completely turned around from our dreams.

The instructor's voice comes in a variety of format...typically it's well-meaning friends and family. Deep in our hearts, we usually know what we need and want. However, when someone else minimizes our dreams and goals, we often rethink and redirect in response. I have been so guilty of this in the past that I shudder now just to think how I relegated my destiny to individuals who shouldn't reasonably be in charge of any meaningful task.

For me, real growth came when I stopped listening to others, exclusively, and started weighing and valuing my own opinions and following them. I am not saying we shouldn't take advice from others. To the contrary, I think good advice should be valued regardless of the source. We simply cannot automatically think that others know more than us, and their ideas and advice are so much better than our personal inclinations. Sometimes it will be true, but not always so we must learn to tell the difference.

If we fail to filter all the input we get from others, one day we will wake up and find ourselves completely turned around from our initial destination. If we allow someone else to sit in the back seat and drive our lives, we will end up where we are directed and not where we want to be. Initially, it may not bother us, but ultimately, we will find ourselves asking, "How on earth did I end up here?" That moment of awakening can be quite frightening but it doesn't have to be. I remember when I was near graduating from college, everyone around me was directing me to go straight to graduate school and I was going along with the program. My cooperation was not the result of personal desire. It was just easier to have someone tell me what to do than to figure out what I was going to do with my life after the security and structure of college.

A few weeks before graduation I started crying uncontrollably in the cafeteria and finally admitted to myself that I didn't want to go to graduate school. I didn't know if it was just then or forever but I knew I was too burned out to function in a graduate program. For the first couple of years out of college, if I didn't like a job, I would think nothing of leaving. I think the people who loved me really worried about me because I was behaving so uncharacteristically and did not seem to have any direction.

I had to feel my way through the fog, making mistakes along the way but I was making my own decisions and whatever the results, I had to hold myself responsible. It was a new and scary feeling and I made some doozies when it came to career and relationship choices. Nevertheless, I survived even when I didn't think I could and I emerged stronger from each experience. There were still the voices in the back seat telling me what to do and sometimes I listened, but more often I didn't.

The familiar is comfortable and who wants to give up comfort? Unfortunately, discomfort often comes with growth. We may experience internal and external discomfort when we decide to take control of our lives. Those who got used to instructing us where to turn will not be happy with our newfound freedom and will make their displeasure known. In spite of that, we just have to keep on hanging on to what we feel is right for us.

Internally, our bodies are likely to go berserk on us, manifesting all kinds of symptoms. Through it all, we just have to hang in there and ask God's guidance for what is right for us. There will even be times when we are tempted to just go back to the old ways and listen to all the voices around us, but we must stay strong, no matter what, because it will be worth it in the end. Wherever we end up, we'll know we got there by our own choice and not someone else's direction.

If someone drives us away from our hopes and our dreams, we cannot blame them because they did it with our permission. Sometimes it is just so much easier to let someone else direct our life's journey, instead of doing our own research, seeking

48

God's guidance, and determining what is best for us. Sometimes others will try to live their unfulfilled dreams through us. The only way they can get away with that plan is if we sit back and allow them to do it. God designed each of us uniquely perfect and never meant for us to be cheap imitations of each other. When we forego our unique purpose in order to let someone else drive us off course, we live our lives as outlines, instead of complete stories.

SONGS:
Patti LaBelle: New Attitude
Diana Ross: I'm Coming Out

SCRIPTURE:
I press on toward the goal to win the prize for which God has called me heavenward in Jesus Christ. Philippians 3:14

WHY NOT ME?

Human beings are basically sympathetic by nature. For example, when we hear about tragedies in other people's lives, we will feel sorry for them sometimes to the point where we will send cash donations or volunteer to help in whatever capacity we can. Sometimes the tragedy is so severe that it keeps us awake at night praying for the victims. However, if the problem or tragedy strikes too close to our homes, our first question is "why me?" Arthur Ashe put it best when he said we shouldn't be asking "why me?", but "why not me?"

Anybody who has known rivers and pain also knows that God never gives us any more than we can bear and He will never leave us. In Isaiah 43:2 He promised, "When you pass through the waters, I will be with you." I view this as one of the most powerful promises in the Bible and one that negates the "why me?" question. You will notice the verse doesn't say "If you pass through the water, I might be with you." The word "when" tells us that stuff is going to happen to you and to me. It will only be a matter of time. Your child will go left, the car will break down, there will be more month than money left over after payday but He will be with you through it all.

If you put all the focus on yourself and wallow in "woe is me" and "why me?" syndromes, you will never hear the message that God has for you and you won't see your way through the storm. Don't ask "why me?"; ask "why not me?". Stay still and the answers will reveal themselves. Remember, you are never alone and if you leave it in God's hand, it will be all right. You are special but not special enough to escape the lessons which were designed for your growth.

Furthermore, there are lessons to be learned as we are going through the fire and the valley. When we learn our lessons well, it is amazing what an impact we can have on the world around us. But if we are busy feeling sorry for ourselves, we will never reach our full potential. When my girlfriend's husband left her for another woman, we expected her to become angry and revengeful, but through it all, she was incredibly calm and gracious. I couldn't take it anymore so, eventually, I asked her, "Didn't you ever feel like going off, tearing up some stuff and getting even?" Her answer summed up what I have been struggling to say. She said, "I can't deny being hurt and angry but if I survive this graciously, then I can be a blessing and encouragement to another woman going through the same thing."

It's not easy to think this way but that is exactly what God wants from us. He wants us to leave our issues in His hands, trust Him, and pay attention. When we cloak ourselves in the blanket of "poor me" and we turn up the volume on the pity party so loud that we can't hear God's word of encouragement, we are robbing ourselves. We need to stop getting in God's way and trying to fix things ourselves because we only make matters worse.

I resolve to let go and let God take over, instead of trying to be in charge, messing things up and then crying "why me?" I have been there and I know the solution is infinitely better when I allow it to come from God. I will also pay attention to the lesson I am supposed to learn from my experiences, instead of wiggling around trying to escape.

SONGS:

Yolanda Adams: The Battle is Not Yours
Mahalia Jackson: His Eye is on The Sparrow

BOOK:

Arthur Ashe: Days of Grace

SCRIPTURE:

For I know the plans I have for you, declares the Lord, plans to prosper you and not to harm you, plans to give you hope and a future. Jeremiah 29:11

Consider it pure joy my brothers, whenever you face trials of many kinds, because you know that the testing of your faith develops perseverance. Perseverance must finish its work so that you may be mature and complete, not lacking anything. James 1: 2-4

Even though I walk through the valley of the shadow of death, I will fear no evil. Psalm 23:4

EX OR WHY?

I don't spend a lot of time watching TV but once in a while I indulge and walk away with some small kernel of value...some tidbit of knowledge or something that makes me laugh. One night I was reading and had the TV on for background but I wasn't really paying attention. However, the standup comedian said something as a joke which I felt was more profound than funny. Her comment was "Some of the men in my life that I refer to as exs should actually be whys?" I chuckled at the time but it gave me cause for some serious thought about my own circumstances.

I look back at some of my own relationships and shake my head in wonder. I wonder what did I see in them for starters. I wonder why I stayed as long as I did. I wonder why I didn't leave. I wonder why I grieved when it was over. The only answer I can give is that I didn't know any better. It's hard to do better when you don't know better.

Psychologists say we develop fixations when some aspect of our development is short-circuited. Consequently, we repeat the same behaviors and habits. It's like learning a new piano piece and hitting a difficult portion. Until you master the bump, you just have to keep playing it over and over again. When you finally get through it, the song will become the masterpiece it was intended to be. There are lessons to be learned from each experience and each relationship. If we miss the lesson, we have to retake the class, oftentimes this remedial relationship is with another person with many, if not all, of the traits of the previous person. Sometimes it's even with the same person.

Until I came to the realization that there are lessons to be

53

learned, I just kept making the same mistakes and wondering why. Some of my relationships were so toxic and unhealthy that, in retrospect, I have an extremely difficult time seeing anything positive in them. However, I have long since come to the realization that the lessons were much deeper than the obvious. This explains why I kept missing them.

One particular ex was so critical that I started to doubt everything about myself and who I was as a person. He criticized my clothes, my hair, my furniture, my cooking, my job, my friends. You name it, he criticized it. You're probably wondering, "Well, why didn't she just leave?" Well, the criticisms or "observations" as he called them, were often ever so subtle and were usually sandwiched between his sense of humor and his zest for life.

In retrospect, I know that the lesson from that particular relationship had to do with self-esteem and self-value. It was a test of what I really believed about myself. I stayed in that relationship because I was in self-doubt and was not ready to commit to the positive things I truly believed about myself. I could not leave until I acknowledged that the messages he was sending me were mutually exclusive to the truth I knew and believed about myself.

I won't take up the space to analyze each of my "ex" but suffice it to say, I am figuring out the "whys?" and it is a very liberating feeling. It will be for you, too, when you stand still and allow the answers to reveal themselves to you and your lessons to be made clear. When you figure out your "whys?", you will graduate from your remedial program, look back at it all and laugh. I have been in your shoes, my sister; I know.

YOU'VE COME A LONG WAY, BABY

When the movie *Waiting to Exhale* opened, I raced to the theater with thousands of other moviegoers in order to be among the first to see it. We all had our reasons for running out to the theaters...some of us wanted to see if the movie was as good as the book; others wanted to see if Whitney could deliver the goods; others wanted to see if Angela could top her Tina; and still others just wanted to see what the hype was all about. My reasons were a little bit of all those, plus I wanted to see if and how my story would be told.

When the camera zoomed in on Angela lying in bed with her red, puffy eyes and tear-stained face, I whispered to myself, "All she's missing is my green robe." The woman was telling my story and that of millions of women across America. Which one of you hasn't been to your own personal well of pain to draw tears because of some man who did you wrong?

If there are sisters out there who have never experienced the grief of unrequited love or love gone wrong, I am not sure what to say to you. I personally went through a period I refer to as my green-robe period. During that time I was living Bernadine's pain as only a teenager could and I wanted to die.

Why else would I stop eating, stop going to class and sit in a corner rocking as if I were autistic and listening to that pitiful Commodores song *Still* over and over again? I wanted to die so the pain would go away but I just cried until I had the dry heaves, my nose bled and my stomach and head hurt. Does that sound like someone who wanted to live?

What was the cause of so much pain? Naturally, it was the man who dumped me and everybody else knew but me. I thought the pain would last forever and I lost all interest in everything. I don't know how my poor roommate put up with me because all I did was cry night and day. I wore my big, fluffy, green robe around the clock. I wouldn't talk to anybody but one of my inner thoughts was that they could bury me in it. Miraculously, I didn't die but the Commodores tape finally broke and my roommate finally spoke her mind.

I slowly came to my senses...a very long drawn out process. I knew I needed to heal and distance had to be part of the healing equation. I changed schools for a while and with the new scenery, the pain began to recede...not fast like the waves at the beach but slowly like my grandfather's hairline. One day I woke up and realized it didn't hurt as much and my foggy daze began to lift.

Summer came and I grew stronger emotionally to the point where I convinced myself I was healed, even if I wasn't sure I was OK. I wouldn't know for sure until I could look <u>him</u> in the eyes and not feel anything. I knew what I had to do so I packed my bags and went back to my old school that fall. My old friends were happy to see me but I knew they were uneasy. They weren't sure if I was going to fall apart again but I knew that I couldn't. I had come too far!

The first time I saw him was anticlimactic...I felt nothing. Well, OK, maybe I felt a little smug because I didn't fall apart and, most importantly, I didn't even want him anymore. My healing had truly begun.

Years later I tell this story and laugh. I laugh because I am no longer the devastated little girl/woman who sat around in that fluffy, green robe crying my heart out. I laugh because so many women share their version of my story...the song of choice may be different but the story is the same. I laugh because I know that no matter how deep the pain, in time we can all look back and tell ourselves "You've come a long way, Baby."

SONGS:

Natalie Cole: Someone I Used to Love
The Winans: Ain't No Need to Worry

SCRIPTURE:

Weeping may remain for a night but rejoicing comes in the morning.
Psalm 30:5b

UNANSWERED PRAYERS

Many times we pray for what we want, when we want it and if God doesn't grant our prayers, we are sorely disappointed. Sometimes we stomp our feet, clench our fists and pout in a way that could teach a card-carrying two-year-old a thing or two. After all, it's only natural. Luke 12:32 tells us that it is our Father's good pleasure to give us the kingdom. So, if we want some desired outcome and we pray for it, why shouldn't we receive it? When God doesn't answer our prayers, we may feel let down or betrayed. Those are the moments that challenge our faith and cause us to question God's wisdom.

When we pray, we are operating from a human agenda and we have human skills. One of the most significant characteristics of God is His omniscience; i.e. His knowledge of everything. My late grandmother would say, "We can only see straight ahead but God sees around the corners." The bottom line is that we are not in God's league so we have to trust Him, even when we are disappointed with the response to our prayers.

If it is God's good pleasure to give us the kingdom, then we can trust that He doesn't want to give us things that are not good for us. When we take this spin on the interpretation, it makes it much easier to say "Lord, this isn't what I prayed for but you know best and I trust your divine guidance".

One of my most vivid experiences with an "unanswered prayer" happened a few years ago. I applied for a position in the New York office for which I was so qualified that my then Director started considering manpower planning combinations to replace me. (That's how sure he was that I would get the job). A few weeks after I interviewed, the hiring vice president's secretary called to schedule a meeting with her boss. I scheduled the meeting for Friday afternoon figuring I could spend the weekend visiting friends in NY and celebrating my new job. That's how sure I was I would get the job.

At the appointed time, I went to Ms. VP's office and we sat and exchanged some pleasantries for a few moments. Eventually, we got into the discussion about the job. I heard her say, "...but I am not going to offer you the position..." After that I saw her lips moving but I didn't hear a sound because I was in shock and heard thunder rolling in my head. Nevertheless, I still had enough of my wits left to smile graciously, shake hands, and utter some appropriate banalities. The truth is I wanted to scream but I held onto my dignity with both hands.

I held myself together until I left the building but I could taste the salty tears in the back of my mouth as I walked to Grand Central Station. By the time the train pulled into the station, I had tears running down my face and I didn't even care. One of the advantages of the NYC subway is that no one really pays attention to anyone, or so I thought.

By the time I got onto the train, I was no longer sniffling. I wasn't bawling out loud but there was no mistaking the fact that I was crying. I was feeling a whole range of emotions--anger, betrayal, and grief, to name a few-- and my tears gave voice to my pain. As the train rumbled through the tunnels leaving Manhattan behind, my frustration escalated and I started sobbing quietly while hanging onto the train pole for dear life and balance. One of the hallmarks of a subway journey is the indifference of the fellow passengers. This isn't always a plus but on that particular day, I was grateful that everyone was ignoring me.

As I wallowed in my grief and anonymity, the man hanging

onto the other side of the pole said in a gentle, soothing voice, "I hope you know that whatever it is, it can't be that bad and it's going to be OK." To me, it was the voice of God telling me to snap out of it. I am not sure what surprised me more...the fact that a stranger spoke to me on the NY subway or the profundity of his words.

Whatever it was, something did snap inside of me and I said to myself, "He's right; this could be a whole lot worse. I still have a job that I love to go back to and I won't have to pack up my house to go pay all those New York taxes." As I continued my positive self-talk, I started to pull myself together and feel better. I said a prayer of acceptance and managed to have a lovely weekend and not give the issue too much more thought.

On Monday I went to see my Director and his first words to me were, "So, when do they want you to start?" When I told him I hadn't gotten the job, he thought I was joking. When he realized I was serious, he offered to call Ms. VP to see what happened. I told him not to bother. (By now I had started to accept what I didn't understand). I told him I held no ill will and would continue to do the best job I was capable of doing.

At that time, I didn't know what the lesson was for me from that experience. Ironically, nine months later the company underwent a major reorganization and the position for which I had cried my eyes out on the NYC subway was eliminated without ceremony. When I heard the news, I felt sad for the person who was in the position but I quietly bowed my head and said, "Thank you, Lord. Now I understand my "unanswered" prayer."

I am sure if you look back in your own life, you can think of occasion after occasion when you wanted something and prayed for it but God saw fit to leave your prayer "unanswered". It may have been years later before you understood the reasons why but when that time came, I am sure it took your breath away. Hold onto that feeling and remember it the next time your prayer is unanswered.

SONGS:

Garth Brooks:	Unanswered Prayers
Aretha Franklin:	Are You Sure Your Prayers Haven't Been Answered?

SCRIPTURE:

But they that wait on the Lord shall renew their strength.; they shall mount up with wings as eagles; they shall run, and not be weary; and they shall walk, and not faint.. Isaiah 40:31

AM I FULFILLING MY PURPOSE?

I was living in the suburbs of Philadelphia during the winter storms of 1994. (The first storm struck on the first Friday in January and it was followed by a weekly series that continued into March). For weeks there was snow and ice on the ground and everything was frozen and brown. It was impossible to imagine that another spring flower would ever break through the ground or that another bird would sing in the tree in front of my kitchen window.

I had several episodes where my car ran off the road, made donuts, or just plain stalled and refused to climb another stubborn, icy hill. The roads remained treacherous as the Department of Transportation ran out of salt and sand and had to go as far as Buffalo, New York to replenish their supply. I was bored out of my mind from being cooped up in the house and I convinced myself that would be the Winter of my Forever. I didn't even feel like going to the mall, so I knew I was in bad shape.

Eventually, the snow and the ice melted and the ground softened. As is the divine plan, the little flowers started to peek out somewhat tentatively at first then with a confident burst of color. The birds came back and started their glorious singing and I was so delighted to hear them that I was actually moved to tears.

I can just hear you now saying "Yeah, yeah, what's the big deal?" or "Well, isn't she just the sensitive type?" To tell the truth, I don't ordinarily pay a lot of attention to nature because, like most people, I just take it for granted that the seasons will follow each other without a lot of drama. The difference, this time, was that the winter lasted so long and was so extreme in temperature and precipitation that it affected me on a deeper level.

When spring finally came, I was no longer the same person I was before. It was as if the voice of God was saying to me, "Don't doubt me no matter how bad things appear to be. I have a plan and my plan will be fulfilled according to my will. You must believe." The experience forced me to confront some basic issues about myself. It forced me to really challenge my faith and question myself about my purpose.

I have always been a believer in the existence of a divine plan or a divine program, but those beliefs were not always in the forefront of my mind. However, I started to face the fact that since God's program will not be short-circuited or tripped up, it must be fulfilled and I needed to start with my own life. I started to challenge my existence and my reason for being here. My questions were along the lines of "Where do I fit in God's plan?", "Am I fulfilling my purpose?" Once I started asking those questions, I knew I could only hear the answers if I tuned out me and started listening to the voice.

I make no claim to knowing the answer and I truly respect those individuals who have found their purpose and have embarked upon a journey of fulfillment. Each day I continue to pray for divine guidance to lead me to my purpose. I may not be there yet but the primary lesson I learned in the winter of 1994 is that God has designed the world and everything in it for a purpose. I continue to seek mine and entreat you to do the same. With our minds and hearts focused, we will each hear our individual message. The message may come from anywhere...a song, a sermon, a book or a bumper sticker. We will only recognize it if we are paying attention. When we do, we must pray for the courage to start moving towards that spring time purpose, even when it seems that the storms of winter will never pass.

SONG: Bette Midler: The Rose

SCRIPTURE:
Before I formed you in the womb, I knew you. Before you were born, I set you apart. Jeremiah 1:5

THE LAYAWAY PLAN

As a child, I was impetuous and impatient and so I hated layaway. Whenever I was getting something new, I wanted it right away, even if it was a new coat in July. I have friends who believe layaway is the greatest invention since pantyhose. I know the idea has its merits but, knowing my personality type, it's simply not well-suited to me. Interestingly, while I have no interest in layaway where merchandise is concerned, I have played a version of the layaway plan with my personal life.

Like most of us, I am pretty intuitive and know when something is not right, but I am also a master game player and will find ways to convince myself that if it's not completely right, it's not that bad so there's no reason to rock the boat. I have stayed in situations that were terribly wrong and woefully unfulfilling but I convinced myself that things would get better. In relationships, it was the man that would act wrong most of the time but would occasionally get up and act right much like the payment on a layaway purchase. In the job, it was the superficial shift of responsibilities and maybe a little title change with a few dollars thrown in for good measure, when nothing had changed materially.

Layaway lacks real commitment. It allows one to keep multiple options open. The merchandise is not on the floor so it is unavailable for other customers to consider. Yet, it has not been fully purchased so the option of voiding the transaction is still very real. In a relationship, it's the ultimate string-along game. There is no future to speak of but the vacant promises keep the merchandise on layaway.

There comes a point when a sister simply has to wake up

and say, "This won't work anymore. You need to either make an outright commitment (purchase) or you need to return the goods to open stock." When you sit on layaway too long, you wake up one day and find that the season has changed and you're not even in style anymore. Your best years have been wasted waiting in vain.

There is no question that change is scary but layaway is a waste of time. It may serve a purpose initially, while we are getting ourselves sorted out. However, eventually the time comes when it does more harm than good. Our society dissuades courageous behavior and instead encourages us to cling to weak excuses and blame others. We must be strong enough to say, "This situation is not working. I am not satisfied and would rather leave and be alone than stay here on layaway with my options limited."

It may mean not having a date on Saturday night but I say date yourself. If you go to the movies solo, the plot won't change and the popcorn will still taste as good. If you go to a concert by yourself, the music will still sound as sweet, if not better, and you can clown to your heart's content. I've seen enough Patti LaBelle and Luther Vandross concerts by myself to know.

SONG: Bob Marley: Waiting in Vain

THE BACK TRACK IS THE EASY ROAD

One morning when I tried to sign on to my computer, I kept getting a message saying there was a problem with my sign-on procedure. After several attempts, I paid closer attention and realized that I was trying to use my old password. I was fascinated because I had changed the password two weeks before and had been using the new one everyday since then. I marveled at the ease with which I slipped back into my old mode. I had used the old password for three months and often typed it in on autopilot. Obviously, the months of repetition had imprinted the old password into my subconscious.

The experience made me to think of all the other times I have initiated changes in my life and managed to slip back to my old ways. One area where I am most guilty is developing and sticking with an exercise routine. I will get all pumped up with my new sneakers and workout clothes and convince myself that I am psyched for my exercise program. I will start out completely gung ho and excited and, because I don't know how to do anything halfway, I jump in with both feet, probably going every day. Next thing I know, I will miss a day but keep going, then I'll miss two then three and so on and, before too long, I have back-tracked to my couch potato ways.

I think that we all make commitments to life changes and honestly mean them when we do. Unfortunately, because the back track is the easy road, it often lures us back and our best-laid plans evaporate in front of us. In such times it is easy to beat up on ourselves and chastise our spirits and souls for failing.

However, the answer lies in accepting our humanity and the fact that our subconscious has the power to pull us back but we have the power to pull out of it. Instead of looking at the cumulative picture, it's best to focus on forcing ourselves back on track and concentrating on one day at a time. There's an old joke that says the best way to eat an elephant is one forkful at a time and the same is true for any endeavor we undertake. It's important that we pray for the strength and energy to maintain our initial enthusiasm because we are programmed to go back to the old ways. When we recognize this, we can rise above it and not berate or punish ourselves.

Staying on track with change is difficult because it forces us to stay conscious and abandon autopilot. From time to time, we will slip back to autopilot because of the inherent ease that the familiar zone brings. However, we are not destined to stay at the old spot (job, man, couch). We have the power to rise above it all, if we will ourselves to achieve a state of consciousness. When we do fall, we need to brush ourselves off and keep on hanging in there just a little bit longer. Eventually, we will be reprogrammed to the point where our new habit or lifestyle becomes the regular state for us and we find ourselves slipping back to that point as our autopilot mode.

Our habits and idiosyncrasies were not formed overnight and the replacement values will not be formed instantaneously either. Our consolation comes from knowing that even if we slip back to the easy track, we have the ability and strength to realign ourselves with our real intentions and start over. As long as we have breath, we have hope and we are not relegated to the back track.

We have far more power over our will than we acknowledge. Two methods that I have found to be particularly effective for me are the buddy system and the written in stone approach. Both methods are based on accountability and they work for me because I don't like to be accountable and come up short. With the buddy system, I either find a partner for my activity or I commit to someone that I am going to honor my commitment. Either way, this person is depending on me and is free to question what I am doing. I keep up my end of the deal because I don't want the embarrassment of acknowledging that I didn't come through. This works for anything whether it's cleaning the house, reading a book, exercising, or working on a project. The trick is to select someone who encourages during periods of success and pushes without putting down during periods of relapse.

The written-in-stone method also works but it requires a more elevated level of commitment than the Buddy System because your accountability is still to yourself. I find that writing a commitment down makes it more potent and, because of my nature, I feel ashamed when I don't follow through. Sometimes laziness and lack of inspiration get the better of me though and I will stare at my written commitment unabashedly and turn the page over. However, when I use this system in the way it was intended, I feel a sense of pride at my accomplishment. I have been known to put goals/progress on the kitchen calendar and give myself stars for honoring my commitments. Even so, sometimes none of my little techniques help and I am pulled back to the back track. When this happens, I remind myself that I am human and there is no disgrace in falling down. The shame would be in not getting up after falling. My prayer is that God will give me the courage to get up and try again after I have fallen.

SONG: Rev. F. C. Barnes: The Rough Side of the Mountain

MISALIGNMENT

Besides filling the gas tank, adding windshield fluid and getting the oil changed, I don't know anything about cars. If I turn the ignition key and the engine starts, the vehicle is fine, as far as I am concerned. When you don't know, you just don't know.

In my ignorant bliss I had been ripping and zipping around town without a care in the world, beyond finding a good parking spot. The car felt fine to me so I had no reason to be concerned. One day I picked up a friend and two minutes after he sat down, he turned to me and said, "Your car needs an alignment. Can't you tell?" I shrugged my shoulders and said, "No, it feels OK to me." He insisted that it was pulling but I couldn't feel whatever I was supposed to be feeling. Therefore, I was in no position to confirm or discount his diagnosis.

While I may be limited in my knowledge of mechanical matters, I had the good sense to listen to good advice. The next day, I took the car to the mechanic and he worked his magic. When I picked it up that evening, the transformation was remarkable. It was like a different vehicle. I was reminded of the line from *Gone With The Wind*, "I was hungry and I didn't even know it."

As I headed down the highway, I started thinking how easy it is to become comfortable and unconcerned with situations that aren't quite right. If things feel fine, then we presume they are. We don't even bother with any kind of close examination. When we don't have a clue what to look for or how to identify red flags, we become complacent in our ignorance.

I believe it is critical that we educate ourselves about the world around us. Education doesn't have to come from a classroom or books. I think we stand to learn so much from our elders and others who have learned from experience. Unfortunately, we sometimes get so caught up in our degrees, credentials and affiliations that we don't have time to spend with older folks. If we take the time to connect with them, they can make us view the world through different eyes, from a perspective we never considered before.

It is true we all learn best from our own mistakes but it is a wise woman who can learn from the mistakes of others. With the insight we gain from our elders, we can do our own diagnosis and recognize when situations are out of alignment. We could prevent many an accident and the ensuing disaster. When we don't know any better, circumstances will seem fine to us but what if they really aren't and we're in dire need of an alignment?

We need to open our minds and take guidance from those in the know. However, we must always evaluate the advice we get to make sure it really is useful. Failing to do this could result in our alignment being thrown even further out of calibration and our finding ourselves exposed to unnecessary danger. There can't be too many situations more pitiful than thinking that our business is all right, when it's on the brink of falling apart.

SONGS:

Whitney Houston:	How Will I Know?
Dianne Reeves:	Better Days

MISSING PIN

I had been living in Texas for several years but had never spent a Christmas here, so I was very excited when I decided to stay in town for the holidays. I went out and bought new decorations for my home and my tree and couldn't wait to put up the tree and get the Christmas theme going. I bought a Christmas tree stand which was designed for four pins, but when I got it home, I realized that it was missing one of the pins. I thought that I could make it work anyway. However, after I put all the effort into screwing in the three pins and putting up the tree, I stepped back to admire my handiwork only to realize that it was just as lopsided as it could be. It occurred to me that the pins could represent different parts of our lives and when we ignore one area, it throws the whole thing off balance.

We live in a fast-paced society which places most of the emphasis on achievement and encourages us to work long, crazy hours, run around taking care of our families and nurturing the world. Sooner or later, some aspect of our balance is bound to shift out of alignment. Either our spiritual world starts to crumble or our physical bodies go into first-degree rebellion, manifesting itself in all kinds of pains, aches, and diseases.

The spiritual, emotional, physical and psychological aspects of our beings are like the pins in the Christmas tree stand. Regardless of how much effort we put into the other areas, if just one aspect is out of sync, the whole thing will become lopsided. The process may be so gradual that we don't even notice it until one day we just snap in one area or another. Black women have a history of taking care of others and we often become so good at our designated role that we neglect to take care of ourselves. We can get away with it for a while but one day our account is going to turn up overdrawn. We have also become so programmed for making excuses that we do it by rote...I'm too busy; I don't have time; I will do it next week, next month, next year, etc.

I know that the area where I fall short, but keep trying, is in the physical. If my body really treated me in response to how I treat it, it would be a sad story. I am a sugar addict unlike any you have ever met. I crave sugar when my hormones start their own private orchestra. I also crave it after meals and at nights. I wish I could say that I withstand the cravings more than I give in to them but it wouldn't be true. I start out with good intentions but, before I know it, I am shoveling down sugar in some form. Hope springs eternal, though, and I have to accept credit for each small victory I gain in my struggle with the sweetened beast.

Exercise is another area where I often have more good intentions than good accomplishments. I have been known to get dressed to go exercise and somehow managed to talk myself out of it. I have started more exercise programs than I can count and I am usually faithful for a while, then I start to skip a day here and there then I up the gap to two or three days. I keep this up over a while and before long the gym shoes are growing dust and the elastic in the workout shorts has turned into dry rot. Heavens only know why I do this since I usually feel so good when I exercise. However, I can find a thousand reasons not to, despite the fact that the reasons to exercise are numerous.

When I am not taking care of the physical, it shows up in other ways. For example, my clothes don't fit right so I'll go out and overspend on new clothes to feel better. When the bills come and I am confronted with my past deeds, I feel bad and my spirit wilts. When I am not in a good mood, I am not pleasant company and my loved ones steer clear of me and I feel even worse. The cycle just gets bigger and bigger and goes round and round and I end up feeling like the Christmas tree.

When I don't spend time in the Word and prayer, my spiritual side starts to starve and events that should bounce off my back affect me deeply. My tongue becomes quicker that it has a right to be and my temper hovers near boiling point. I become easily annoyed and I am not a pleasant person to be around. For as much as my loved ones don't want to be around me, I don't want to be around them either. When I get that way, I know what I have to do to fix myself but prevention would have been so much easier than repair. I am so grateful for God's love despite the reality that is me.

When all the areas are properly aligned, I feel like I am floating. I feel good physically; I am in a good mood; I make the people around me laugh and they enjoy my company. I feel grounded in God's love and it is manifested in all my interactions. Life becomes good. Unfortunately, the misalignment happens more often than it should but I am far more alert and I am making a diligent effort to have all my pins in place.

When you are feeling overwhelmed and out of sorts, it's important to remind yourself that the situation does not make you inadequate or unlovable. You are not alone in what you are going through. Others have been there and survived and so will you. The alignment trick comes from reminding yourself that if you don't take care of your "pins", you will be no good to anyone else and are more likely to become a burden to those around you.

SONG:

Allen and Allen: Lost Without You

SCRIPTURE:

What good will it be for a man if he gains the whole world, yet forfeits his soul? Matt. 16:26

KNOW YOUR VALUE BEFORE YOU ACCEPT THE OFFER

I am an avid collector of dolls and find myself with a collection which range in price from less than a dollar to several hundred dollars. Clearly, there is some element which determines the value of these dolls. However, the determining factor is not always well-known or easily recognized. Recently, I went to a garage sale and my eyes zoomed in on a doll I had been longing for for some time. I asked the man how much he wanted for it and he said, "Make me an offer." I made what I thought would have been an insultingly low offer expecting him to laugh in my face and then I would have laughed too and said, "I was only joking." To my amazement, he said "Sounds good to me."

While this story is not unusual, it is certainly illustrative. Stories like these are rampant because one person doesn't know the value of what he has to offer. Unfortunately, similar events happen in our personal and professional lives. As Black women, there are so many messages we receive from the society around us aimed at discounting and devaluing our worth that sometimes we unconsciously absorb them and lose track of who we are. This is best evidenced when we leave it up to others to "make us" an offer, be it in relationships, jobs or whatever.

Sometimes we come into a relationship so hungry for love, affection, validation, etc., that we set very low expectation

76

standards for the other person or worse yet, we don't set any standards at all and anything goes. Doing this is the same as saying, "I don't think I am worth that much so make me an offer in terms of your time, your energy, your respect, your commitment, etc." We are in dangerous territory when we do this because we ignorantly give up our treasures, just as that man handed me that valuable doll for less than lunch money.

I have had to change my approach in a lot of areas in my life and I sometimes look back and wonder just who I was when I made the decisions I made in the past. I have forgiven myself for the wrong career and personal decisions I made when I didn't know better. I acknowledge that some of the decisions I made would be considered stupid by some people and particularly so by the person I am today. However, the measure of growth, for me, comes from knowing that when I knew better, I did better and made better choices. I bestow more value on myself today and my expectations from those around me reflect it. I didn't get here overnight but today I take pride in the fact I no longer expect others to make me an offer. I know my worth in God's eyes and my own and I am not prepared to compromise or haggle. I Peter 2:9 tells me I am of a "royal priesthood, a chosen nation." That does not sound like a negotiable value to me.

For any deal to be successful, it helps if each party knows the value of the merchandise. Sometimes our mistake doesn't just come from not knowing our own value; it also comes from overvaluing what we are getting. A good example is the person who buys the knockoff designer bag at the flea market and brags, "I only paid one hundred bucks and poor Mary paid three hundred at the boutique." Never mind that the bag is barely worth ten dollars! She was willing to pay her good money for junk thinking she was getting a bargain. I know that I have done the same thing in matters far more important than a purse.

Sometimes a person or situation looks like and smells like the real thing and can easily pass inspection unless we know what signals to look for. Unfortunately, many times we don't know what to look for and sometimes we are so taken in with the superficial that we are blinded to serious character defects. Only after we have blown our last dollar (emotional, financial, psychological) do we wake up with the Home Alone look thinking, "Oh my goodness, what have I done? Why didn't I see it? How could I have been so stupid?"

It helps to set up your own definition of quality in whatever circumstance you are trying to evaluate. I find that when I have guidelines established in advance, I can assess defects more clearly and make more sensible decisions. When I don't, I ignore warning signals or I rationalize them away and I end up losing in some way or the other.

I have been on job interviews where every person I encountered in the hallway looked miserable and no one smiled. Nevertheless, when the recruiter souped up the job description and showcased the perks, I chose to ignore everything else and jump in, only to regret it later when I found myself to be one of those people walking around looking constipated. I have gotten involved in relationships where the man drove the right car, had the right job and wore the right cologne but didn't get along with his family or had no close friends. Even with a degree in psychology, I chose to ignore what was so obvious in hindsight and paid dearly for my carelessness.

In order not to be taken, we must know our own worth and

be steadfast in our definition of value. This does not guarantee that we won't make mistakes but it will surely reduce the likelihood. At no point can we allow our value to be set by some external force. As precious heirs of God, we must remember who we are and whose we are. When we are conscious of our worth, our boundaries change. We will treat ourselves differently in a way that shows the world that we value and respect ourselves. In return, others will be less inclined in their attempts to mark us down and toss us in the clearance bin.

SCRIPTURE:

Don't you know that you yourselves are God's temple and the God's Spirit lives in you? If anyone destroys God's temple, God will destroy him. For God's temple is sacred, and you are that temple. I Corinthians 3:16-17

SELF-ACCEPTANCE

I wrote the following poem Christmas 1998 as a word gift for our women's ministry. I think the message is worth sharing so here goes:

MY BEAUTIFUL SISTER, YOU ARE OK

Everywhere you look the world tells you what's wrong with you:
You're too short, too tall, too skinny, too fat, too dark, too light.
I just want to remind you that you are all right.
You come from a royal priesthood and a prince died just for you.
You must be pretty special considering all He went through.

They try to fix you up with a bottle.
They say, "try the lotion, the potion, the pill or the sip."
Sister Girlfriend, let me give you a little tip:
You are wondrously and marvelously made and
Nothing from a bottle can make you a better grade.
Your beauty comes not from the wearing of gold or from the weave or the braids.
It comes from your inner glow which never fades.

In this holiday season, stay strong and prayerful.
remember, you are too blessed to be stressed,
Because God's got your back.

SCRIPTURE:
Charm is deceptive, and beauty is fleeting; but a woman who fears the Lord is to be praised. Proverbs 31:30

TURN OFF THE AUTOPILOT

The other day I went to an event downtown and had to park in the theater garage. The woman collecting the money looked hot and sweaty but she was wearing some beautiful earrings. I complimented her on how lovely they were and her response was to suck her teeth, sigh and say, "You can put it anywhere you want to." I stared at her with a puzzled look and asked her, "What are you talking about?" She glared at me and asked "Didn't you ask me where you could park?" I shook my head and said "No, I did not. I actually complimented you on how nice your earrings were but I guess you heard what you have been programmed to hear."

I know that I have been equally guilty of going on autopilot myself but seeing it up close in someone else made me realize just how harmful the habit can be. Everyone feels special when someone pays them a sincere compliment, but in this lady's case she couldn't hear the compliment because she was past the point of listening. What have I cheated myself from receiving when I am on autopilot? Maybe it's the smile of a stranger, a rainbow in the sky, the beauty of the flowers, the singing of the birds, the radiance of a sunset or the beauty of a butterfly. Those are the little things that come to mind but I have probably missed even bigger gifts of every ilk because I was zipping by on autopilot with no level of consciousness.

I pray that God will keep me in a state of consciousness

where I can appreciate the gifts around me in all their forms. More importantly, I pray that my eyes will be open to need around me in all its manifestations. No longer do I just want to walk on by and not make a difference. I know in my heart that the times when I have ignored or blocked out need around me were not based on heartlessness or indifference, but being on autopilot and being oblivious.

I think real living encompasses the good, the bad and the neutral around us. When we switch off the consciousness button, we rob ourselves of the opportunity to experience life fully. The occurrence is comparable to walking through a beautiful botanical garden with blindfolds. We may smell the aroma of the flowers but our blindness deprives us of the full experience of all the garden has to offer. We owe it to ourselves not to short change our lives.

My prayer for you, my sister, is that you, too, will go through life with your eyes open and your senses heightened. This life is a gift and we are meant to enjoy it and make a positive difference in the world around us. It's very difficult to do this, if we are stuck on fast forward and operating on autopilot.

SONG:

The Dells: Open Up My Heart

DO YOU HAVE ENOUGH LIGHT?

A bunch of us recently went to Cancun on a working trip and there was a lot of anticipation and excitement leading up to the journey. Unfortunately, when we got there, we experienced several minor mix-ups and inconveniences and it was very late when we finally got to our rooms. Needless to say, we were exhausted and pretty much crashed. The next morning I was pleasantly surprised to discover that we actually had a balcony overlooking the luscious Caribbean Sea. As I sat out there meditating and enjoying the fresh air, it occurred to me that I had overlooked the beauty the night before because I was not in the right frame of mind to enjoy or appreciate it.

Sometimes in our day-to-day lives we miss so much beauty around us because we are not in the right frame of mind and our inner eyes are not open. We overlook the look of awe on a child's face when she sees a butterfly; we ignore the butterfly; we can't smell the air after the rain; we miss the smile of a stranger. We are blind to the colors in the rainbow. We never notice the sunset. The sunrise annoys us. These aren't the big gifts of life; they are the little goody gifts, somewhat akin to finding a Hershey's kiss on your pillow or a five-dollar bill in your jacket pocket from the last time you wore it. They don't make the earth move but they sure shift your mind in the right direction.

When I allow the world to mangle my spirit, all I can think of is retreat. However, if I stop to look around me as I am making my escape, I see so much joy that the big, bad world doesn't matter. It takes the right light to see the beauty around us and that light has to come from within. If we close our eyes in an attempt to block out what's ugly, we will also overlook what's lovely. When we are going through periods of distress and the world has beaten us to a pulp, we have to seek encouragement from positive people who can help us to see the good in our circumstances.

Bitter, angry people obscure our vision. If our light is dim to begin with, they just create more darkness. They will point out all that is negative and discouraging. Because they are stumbling around in the dark, they have become accustomed to the low visibility. If you try to let in the light, it hurts their eyes. Don't let that hold you back—move towards the light so you can see better. When your immunity is down and you are doubting yourself, it is especially dangerous to be around negative people. They will infect you with their dismal outlook and, before long, you will not have the light to see anything positive. The next thing you know, their view will be your view too and the world will become a dismal, hopeless place. I say run from negative people like they are carrying bombs because they are and you will blow up in the aftermath.

SONGS:
Walt Whitman: Perfect Praise (How Excellent)
Beau Williams: Wonderful

SCRIPTURE:
Put your trust in the light while you have it, so that you may become sons of light. John 12:36

DON'T LET YOUR LACE ROT

Celebrity deaths usually do not affect me in a deep way but I remember being completely shaken when Princess Diana and Flo Jo died. After all, they were both so young, so beautiful and so full of life and their deaths were just so sudden. There was no mental or emotional preparation for the news. I never met either woman but, because I worked out to Flo Jo's video and she was so inspirational and encouraging, I felt some sense of connection to her. Princess Diana had been a cultural icon for most of my adult life. There was something about their glamour which deluded a part of the mind into thinking that death couldn't find them, even though the rational part knew better. The lesson that their deaths brought home for me is the necessity of appreciating the joys of life (family, friends, nature, etc.) now because there's no predicting the midnight hour.

I grew up in a household where I was encouraged to save things for "special occasions", so I got minimal use out of the items I valued the most. I especially remember a big talking doll I received when I was about eight years old. I was discouraged from playing with her because the grown folks thought I would damage her. As a result she sat high upon a shelf just looking down through her long silky lashes. On a "special" occasion I was allowed to play with her and the first thing I did was pull the string in her back to engage the talking mechanism. Unfortunately, while she sat on her perch over the course of time, the string had dry rotted. One pull from my little hand

and the string disintegrated and that doll never spoke again. In the end, she suffered her loss of speech as much from sitting upon the shelf as from me playing with her.

I also remember my dressy shoes being saved for special occasions but when such occasions arose, I had outgrown them. Imagine the irony of never having enjoyed them. Unfortunately, this happens in grown up lives all the time--we save cherished items for special occasions and never get to enjoy them for a variety of reasons. Once I heard a motivational speaker tell a story of how his grandmother brought all kinds of beautiful lace from Italy but kept it all locked up in a trunk waiting for a special occasion. The lace stayed in the trunk for about 35 years without being used. Eventually, Grandma died and when they opened the trunk, all the beautiful pieces of lace just crumbled in their hands because of dry rot. How sad that a thing of infinite beauty would waste away unused because there was never an occasion "special" enough to use it.

There is so much beauty in our lives that we save up needlessly instead of enjoying. Sometimes it's a special dress or sweater or a special perfume or the "good" jewelry. When we eventually decide to wear the dress or sweater, it's too small or out of style or, horror of horrors, has a moth hole at the most conspicuous spot that cannot be camouflaged. The perfume becomes slightly "off" and has just a hint of scented bug spray to it. In the end, we've saved the cherished only to lose it without enjoyment.

Some people think that you if you use the "special" stuff every day, they won't be "special" on appropriate occasions, but I completely disagree. If anything, I think it makes every day special. Isn't that a wonderful thought? Life is way too short with no promises of that "special" occasion. Whatever the symbolic lace is in your life, don't let it rot. Use it up until it falls apart from over use and you have your memories to fall back on but don't let it die the death of storage. I don't think any of us will lay on our death bed thinking "Gee, I wish I hadn't used the good china so often or I wish I hadn't worn the life out of my favorite dress."

Life was meant to be lived to its fullest and we cannot accomplish this by putting boundaries on little pleasures. I am not telling you to take your 401K and run off to Rio (although that may be the right thing for some of us). I am talking about enjoying the sweet little pleasures that life offers instead of storing them up. Maybe that means brown bagging last night's leftovers and using today's lunch money to buy fresh flowers or doing your own manicure and springing for a pedicure. Hey!

SONG: Andrae Crouch & Disciples: It Won't Be Long

SCRIPTURE: Luke 12: 16-21   (The Parable of the Rich Fool)

Jetola E. Anderson-Blair

PMS

For some reason, when a woman speaks her mind or asserts herself in any way, our society is in the habit of snickering and making sly references to it being "that time of the month." Of course, this is an unfair characterization but, even at the dawn of the new millennium, America is still uncomfortable with strong women who don't behave by the script. On the other hand, sometimes it really is "that time of the month" and the issues related to it are no laughing matters. Only a woman who has experienced the bloating, uncontrollable cravings, nausea and elephant cramps that come with PMS and menstruation can understand.

Because some women don't experience the symptoms, they join in the snicker brigade and denigrate the sisters whose lives are often put on hold during that time. Until my late teens, my cycle was basically a nonevent; it came and went without a whimper. Somewhere into my early twenties I developed the kind of cramps which I dubbed elephant cramps because I thought they just might kill an elephant. My doctor put me on one kind of pain killer after another and as soon as I derived any comfort, my body would get used to the dosage and it had to be increased. This scenario continued for years and I developed additional symptoms such as backaches, nausea and light sensitivity. I had what seemed like a lifetime prescription for Anaprox® and I had resigned myself to the fact that prescription drugs would always be a part of my life.

In 1995 I went to hear an herbalist lecture on the effect of diet on our health and how much of what ails us can be remedied with natural products instead of drugs. Knowing how long I had experienced my problem and being acquainted with several women similarly-situated, I did not   have an open mind. I expected the lecture to be rubbish and I was not prepared to be impressed in any way. Not being one to hide my feelings well, the lecturer picked up on my vibes and addressed me at the end of the lecture.

He approached me and said, "I can see you have a lot of doubt; which part of what I said do you have the biggest trouble with?" His statement about dairy products being a contributing factor to most female health problems simply had not set well with me because I had a very personal relationship with Häagen Daz® ice cream.   Furthermore, my day just couldn't start without a bowl of cereal and let's not even talk about the thing I had going with strawberry cheesecake and baked macaroni and cheese. What he was saying was hard for me to handle and I would have preferred to just block it out than to entertain the idea of giving up so many staples of my life. I told him I had a difficult time seeing the connection between my monthly pain and my dairy consumption.

I guess he must have heard my argument a thousand times before because he was completely unfazed by anything I had to say. Instead of debating me, he simply suggested that I give up dairy products for thirty day (roughly the equivalent of one menstrual cycle). I figured I would prove him wrong so I agreed. It was a difficult feat and sometimes the cravings got so bad that I was ready to abandon the whole idea. Anyway, before I knew it, the thirty days had passed and lo and behold, I did not experience any pain or other symptoms and, for the first time in fifteen years, I did not require medication.

A less stubborn person would have become a believer but

not Hard Headed Hannah. I decided that it was just a fluke and did not prove anything. To support my argument, I went without dairy for another thirty days and again I had no symptoms. At this point, I started to believe that there may be something to this theory but I was not fully convinced. Just to be sure, the third month I resumed eating all my favorite goodies and, naturally, when my period started, I had all my old symptoms: pain, bloating, nausea and irritability.

The experience was an eye opener for me even though a part of me remained skeptical. In my disbelief, I kept going back and forth with my dairy consumption and each time I indulged, I paid the price in pain. Eventually, I decided that as much as I loved ice cream and cheesecake, I loved being pain free more. It has not been an easy road but this has been a life-changing event for me and I simply wish someone had clued me in to this sooner. Subsequently, I have read numerous publications which make the connection between health and dairy products. I am only one person and would not dare speak for the world but I would recommend that each person tests the theory for herself and then make her decision accordingly.

I remember that one of the biggest struggles for me with this concept was that I thought giving up dairy products meant that I would have to give up the food which used milk and cheese as ingredients. It turns out there are various lines of soy, rice and oats substitutes which taste so good you can hardly tell the difference. The only thing missing these days is the pain but you know that I am not missing it. I don't always walk the straight and narrow but each year I am getting better and the change is becoming more of a lifestyle than something I occasionally do in an attempt to repair damage I inflict upon myself. I don't know what your experience will be, if you try this. However, I can say that I have never felt better and I still marvel at the change.

SONG: James Brown: I Feel Good

SCRIPTURE:
Mark 5: 25-34 (The woman with the issue of blood)

BOOK:
Llaila Afrika: Nutricide

Jetola E. Anderson-Blair
LET GO OF THE PENNY

We once had a guest minister at our church and at the end of his sermon he told a story which had a very deep impact on me and forced me to confront some issues about myself. The story was about a woman who had a very rare and expensive vase which she repeatedly told her son not to touch.

One day she came into the room to find her son with his hand stuck in the vase. Naturally, her first concern was for his well-being, so after trying various options, she had to resort to breaking the vase in order to free his hand. When she broke the vase, she realized that little Johnny's hand was tightly clenched into a fist. When he opened his hand, she saw that he had been holding onto a penny. If he had let go of the penny, he would have been able to slip his hand out of the vase effortlessly. Instead, the rare vase had to be sacrificed to save the penny. Whew!

That story made me confront myself about the times I clung to things of little value and blocked my blessings. It's the time when I chose to stay at a job I was comfortable with, even though I wasn't learning anything new instead of taking on a new job on the other side of town because I didn't want to drive "all the way over there." It's the time I didn't take a course because it clashed with something trifling on my schedule. It's the decision not to take the swimming class because it would mess up my hairdo.

Sometimes we place too much value on things that are not important and then we turn around and let them get in the way of greater more important gifts. It is not easy but we have to challenge ourselves to be strong and pray for a spirit of discernment so that we can tell the difference between the diamonds and the cubic zirconia in our lives. We will stumble and make mistakes along the way but as long as we make it our life's mission to seek the truth and the greater good in our lives, we still have hope.

Everything in our life comes along for a purpose and a season and sometimes we hold on long after the purpose has been fulfilled and the usefulness has served it tenure. In many ways I am like a child with my need to cling to the comfortable and the familiar. However, if I look back and evaluate my life, I realize that my most triumphant moments have arisen from the times when I opened up my hands, let go of the familiar and the comfortable, threw my arms in the air and embraced the unknown. (Moving to Houston with the phone number of a friend of a friend in my wallet and not knowing a soul, was one such moment.) As much as I know this and as much courage as this knowledge brings me, it is still not easy. Fear can immobilize me but sometimes that same fear can catapult me into heights I never imagined.

I have to remind myself that there is a whole new world waiting for me but it won't come to me; I have to run towards it. If I dig my feet in and cling to the familiar, I will miss what is waiting for me. I have pledged to myself that I will not sacrifice the treasure of the unknown for the low currency of comfort and familiarity. This is an easy resolve to make on paper but I know that when I am faced with the reality of letting go, it will be quite difficult. Instead of jumping in with my eyes clenched tightly, I will test the waters with one toe and let go one finger at a time.

All the trite expressions come to mind: "You can't get to home with your foot on base.", "The longest journey begins with single step.", etc. However, instead of devaluing them and smirking, I am going to take them to heart and apply them to my mindset. I am looking forward to my growth and I hope you are looking forward to yours.

SONG:

Regina Belle and Peabo Bryson: A Whole New World

SCRIPTURE:

For God did not give us a spirit of timidity, but a spirit of power, of love and of self-discipline. 2 Timothy 1:7

YOU DESERVE MORE THAN CRUMBS

Black women are raised to take care of others—our families, our friends and our communities. Certainly this is a good thing and, for the most part, it makes us feel good about ourselves. There are few things in life that measure up to the pleasure of seeing your loved ones happy and cared for. However, when this loving and caring for others come at the expense of self-care, the results can be downright catastrophic. I think the character Mama Jo in the movie *Soul Food* best exemplifies what I am trying to say.

I remember going through a stress management class where the instructor told us to think of each new day a big, beautiful pie, sliced up in equal pieces. For each obligation we must honor we remove a slice of the pie. At the end of the exercise, each of us had divided and distributed our pies until there were only crumbs left on the plates. When she asked us to raise our hands if we had shared out a slice for ourselves, not one hand went up in that auditorium. It was a shocking but telling exercise.

We are taught that it is selfish to think of ourselves first and we take this message to heart. However, thinking of and caring for ourselves is exactly what we need to do before we can fully and completely give to others. Somehow we must replenish our own wells or eventually there will be nothing left either for our loved ones or ourselves. This idea is so foreign to some of us that we break out in a cold sweat at the very thought. As with anything new and uncomfortable, it will take time and initially will require baby steps. With practice we will become much more

95

comfortable and convincing in our new posture.

If we allow everyone around us to take a can from our cupboards and never put anything back and we never replenish them, eventually the cupboard will be the demo for the old Mother Hubbard story. The objective here is not to forget about others and their needs but to make our needs as important as those around us. If we don't take care of our needs up front, we will find that there isn't enough, time, energy or resources to address them at the end of the line. This represents a big mindset change but it is so critical. By making our needs important, we equip ourselves to better fulfill all the roles we have in life—daughters, wives, mothers, sisters, friends, etc.

We must take care of ourselves and give ourselves the honoring and pampering we deserve. There are so many little ways that we can replenish our cupboards which cost little or no money. Some ideas that come to mind include taking a walk in the park, buying yourself flowers, lighting a couple candles, soaking in the tub, getting a massage, writing in a journal, renting that movie that no one wanted to see with you, going to the movies by yourself, putting on your favorite CD and dancing by yourself, exercising, buying a blouse or a scarf in a color that is outside your everyday palette, setting a fancy table on a Tuesday night (so what if you're only serving spaghetti?), calling someone who believes in you and loves you unconditionally.

Somehow it seems that if you have a slice of pie for yourself, you will be less likely to be hungry or resentful and, ultimately, will have more of yourself to give to others. If we simply give and give and never take any time for ourselves, eventually there'll be nothing left because we will fall apart inside and just become walking shells. Everyone of us deserves better than that. God did not mean for us to subsist on crumbs. Life was meant to be lived abundantly not just for those we care about but for us as well.

BOOK: Debrena Jackson Gandy: Sacred Pampering Secrets

SONGS:

Betty Griffin Keller:	Eagles Wings
Betty Griffin Keller:	Satisfy Your Soul

Jetola E. Anderson-Blair

EVERYBODY NEEDS AN ANCHOR

Recently, I was helping a friend hang some drapery and we kept running into a problem. Not long after we hung them, the nails would become loose and start to pull away from the wall, making the drapes hang lopsided. Eventually, we decided to take down the drapes and leave the valance hanging. I mentioned the problem to my husband and he told me that the wall was hollow and in order for the drapery rod to stay put, we would need to anchor it. Now I know a lot about a lot of things but this was foreign terrain for me; my passport had never been stamped on this subject.

Anyway, he patiently explained to me what we needed to do and I went off to the hardware store to get the necessary supplies. Even after I got the material, I wasn't sure that I had a clear grasp of how it would work. Later, he met me at my friend's house and went about installing the anchors. When he was finished, he attached the brackets and they never so much as budged, much less wobble. I was fascinated and couldn't help but think how we each go through experiences which make us rock and wobble and sometimes fall apart.

I started reflecting on experiences in my own life which rocked my world (bad relationships, betrayal, bad decisions, job loss, death of loved ones, etc.) and wondered how I came through with a sound mind. I remember feeling fragile and vulnerable and crying seemingly endlessly. It took so little to take me to the brink and dunk me into a funk—hearing a song on the radio or smelling certain fragrances. At the time, I didn't have a clue how I got through it or what kept me from totally collapsing and disintegrating before my very eyes.

With the benefit of hindsight and spiritual growth, I now recognize that God was my anchor, even when I didn't know it. I rocked and wobbled and blew in the wind but something kept me holding on even when I didn't feel like it. I know it was the prayers of loved ones and God's undiluted grace which kept me going. There were times when I pretended to function and eventually the act became real.

No matter what you are going through (you may be pulling out of the wall like that drapery rod) just hang in there with the conviction that somebody bigger and stronger than you is anchoring you. You may recall that in the crucifixion Christ submitted and said, "Father into your hands I commit my spirit." When we're going through our whippings, sometimes we need to stop struggling and submit our situation to the power that can anchor us and keep us grounded.

SONGS:

| Douglas Miller: | My Soul Has Been Anchored |
| Mississippi Mass Choir: | Your Grace and Mercy |

SCRIPTURE:

Fear not, for I have redeemed you; I have summoned you by name, you are mine. When you pass through the waters, I will be with you; and when you pass through the rivers, they will not sweep over you. When you walk through the fire, you will not be burned; the flames will not set you ablaze. For I am the Lord your God, the Holy one of Israel, your savior. Isaiah 43: 1-3

Jetola E. Anderson-Blair

SUCCESS IS THE BEST REVENGE

As long as you are alive there will be someone out there to put you down in one way or another. They will discourage you and poke holes in your dreams every chance they get. When you face this kind of spirit stealing every day, it is natural to give in to it a little bit at a time, until one day you wake up thinking you are inadequate and your gifts have no value. On the other hand, you could use the put-downs and the discouragement as the force that catapults you to heights which would make your naysayers dizzy.

There's an old saying that says that living well is the best revenge and that just may be so. However, I contend that success is the best revenge. There is nothing more gratifying than watching your critics and dream stealers eat their words. I know a young man who could not get into the Honor Society when he was in high school because his grades were not up to the mark. Today he is a successful writer and computer consultant and he was recently invited back to his alma mater to give a speech to the Honor Society. Can you spell irony?

I am sure the school thought they were finished with him when he marched down the aisle on graduation day. On the other hand, they had high hopes for the "honor" graduates and expected to see them again as they made their mark on the world. This young man could have accepted his prescribed lot but he chose not to. Instead, he decided to "show them" and he did so with magnificent style. At the rate he's going, I wouldn't be surprised if the school ended up naming a wing after him.

If you look into the backgrounds of some of our brightest and most famous stars, you will find that they overcame great obstacles and much criticism to reach where they are. Sure it is wonderful to have someone in you corner rooting for you and telling you that you are capable and can do anything. This strengthens your dream and your resolve and helps you on your way but we aren't always that fortunate. The naysaying, dream-stealing experience is probably more typical for most of us. While they may mean it for evil, you can turn it around and make it something good. Your success will be the best revenge.

You have the power of choice—you can either let your dreams and goals drain out to sea or you can fill them with the helium of determination and hard work and make them soar. When you look back, you will have no choice but to smile and give thanks. Things don't have to end up the way they were intended. You can't change someone's intentions but you can change your reaction and your results. When all is said and done, your success will be your best revenge.

SONGS:
Dottie Peoples: For My Good
Sounds of Blackness: Don't Let Nothin' Keep You Down

SCRIPTURE:
The stone the builders rejected has become the capstone; the Lord has done this and it is marvelous in our eyes. Psalm 118: 22 – 23

You intended to harm me, but God intended it for good, to accomplish what is now being done. Genesis 50:20

Jetola E. Anderson-Blair

GIVE ME MY ROSES WHILE I'M ALIVE

When my grandmother was alive, she used to say, "Give me my roses while I'm alive; don't throw them on me when I can't see or smell." I used to think that was such a strange thing for her to say but as I got older, it made much more sense to me. Her point was brought home to me very vividly when i recently attended a funeral where the flowers just about covered the whole church. I remember thinking that the deceased would really have appreciated them, if only she could see and smell them.

In our busy lives we get so caught up in all that we have to do that we often don't even bother giving roses (literal or symbolic) to those we love. We never take the time to tell them we love them or let them know how much the little things they do mean to us. I think this is a big contributor to the drama we see at some funerals. It's the knowing that we never let the person know how we felt and that the opportunity is permanently lost that sends our grief into overdrive. I know that today I am still racked with remorse that a friend of mine died suddenly, and the last time I saw her I was on the phone and too busy to talk to her. It doesn't matter how much I tell her family I valued her; she never heard it so how was she to know it?

Every day we have numerous opportunities to spew roses on those we love. We must take advantage of those chances because in the wink of an eye they can be taken away for good and no amount of flowers or graveside tears will give us another real chance. We must take the time out to genuinely express our love to those we cherish so that if they pass on before we do, we can at least have the clear conscience of knowing that they knew for sure how we felt. How is it that in death we will find hundreds of dollars to buy roses the deceased will never see or smell, but we can't buy a five-dollar bouquet from the guy on the corner? Stop to think about it; which one will your loved one be able to appreciate more?

In life there are so many opportunities to express our appreciation and love for those around us. However, we usually don't because we're too busy and we think we can always do it tomorrow. We need to remind ourselves that today is all we have. Tomorrow is hoped for but neither promised nor guaranteed. If we give our roses today, we get to see and enjoy the recipient's response, which makes us feel good. If we wait for tomorrow, who knows?

SONGS:

Willie Nelson: You Were Always On My Mind
Stevie Wonder: I Just Called to Say I Love You
Stevie Wonder: These Three Words

Jetola E. Anderson-Blair

DON'T BLOCK THE BLESSINGS!

God has made all kinds of promises to us, including the promise of limitless blessings. Sometimes we don't receive the blessings He has in store for us because we block them. I think one of the easiest ways to block our blessings is by not appreciating what we have and envying what others have. Everything we have is a gift from God, but sometimes we don't appreciate what we have because, no sooner than we get ours, that a faster, shinier, bigger, better one comes on the market. Instead of being grateful for what we have, we start lusting after the upgrade. That's blessing blocking!

Another way we block our blessings is by crying poor mouth over what we do have. I know a woman who works every moment of overtime that is offered to her. She forgoes time with her friends and will not do anything other than work. Yet this person cries poor mouth over the smallest decision she has to make. To hear her bicker over a few dollars, one would be led to believe that she was just scraping and getting by when she's not. When we clench our fists, we can't receive anything else. That's blocking the blessing!

The bible to tells us to give thanks in everything, but if we focus on what's missing or what's wrong, we can't appreciate what's there and what's right. If we don't take care of what we do have, why should God give us more? We will sit up all night and pray for a new car, bigger house, more money, etc., even when we are not good stewards over what we already have. We are stewards of everything we have and God charges us to take

104

care of and make good use of that which is in our possession. Why should we get a new car when the one we have is filthy inside and out, plastered with fast food containers, newspapers, magazines and other junk? If we never take care of the scheduled maintenance, and things snap, crackle and pop on us, whose fault is that? God has blessed us with transportation (the real need), so if we mess up what we have, we are blocking the blessing.

Granted, our society encourages us to keep up with the Joneses and to link our self-esteem and self-worth with our material possessions. Somehow what we have is never enough because someone else will always have "the new and improved" one and we want what they have or we want to have the next upgrade so that what we have is better. Envying what others have is like standing under a car port when the blessings are raining down.

We block our blessings with our thoughts, our words and our actions. It is not God's desire to withhold good things from us, but when we behave in an unworthy manner, we block our own blessings. When we see blessings raining down on others, instead of wondering why they are getting the good stuff, we need to look at home and honestly ask ourselves how we are blocking the blessings. The answers will surprise us but the good thing is that we have the assurance that God wants to bless us, so our situation will only last for a while. We have more control than we give ourselves credit for.

SONG:

Patti LaBelle: Don't Block the Blessing

SCRIPTURE:

"Test me in this", says the Lord Almighty "and see if I will not open the flood gates of heaven and pour out so much blessing that you will not have room enough for it." Malachi 3: 10b

GET OUT OF GOD'S WAY!!

I must confess that my greatest strength is also my greatest weakness. I like to be in charge because "I know the right way to do everything and nobody could ever do it as well as me." Therefore, delegation is not my thing. You may be the same way or you may know someone just like that and you know that God will not put up with that kind of attitude for too long. I remember when my prayers were really instructions to God, as if He were personal butler or gofer. They went something like, "Lord, I want you to do this, this and this and I want it done by such a time." I actually had the nerve to wonder why He didn't do as I had demanded and had no trouble telling Him how disappointed I was.

It took age and spiritual growth to open up my eyes but when I did, oh what I sight I beheld! I now realize how I was just getting in God's way with my little bossy self. In Jeremiah 29:11 He said, "I know the plans I have for you; plans to prosper you and not to harm you, plans to give you hope and a future." Nevertheless, I convinced myself that either God didn't have a plan or His plan was not the right one. As a result, I would take things into my own hands and make decisions with no guidance or direction. To tell the truth, sometimes my misguided decisions turned out OK and that was just enough to convince me that I had it going on. Ah!, but oh the times when I got a whipping and didn't know which way to turn. That was my little stubborn doing too.

As I have gotten older and have grown in my spiritual walk, I now realize that things are just so much easier when I submit to

107

God's will and let Him direct my path. In the old days I had to understand it or was not going to cooperate. Now I understand that, while some things are simply beyond my comprehension, God has everything in control. Accepting that has allowed for less of a struggle and less of a whipping based on stubbornness.

Think of when you were a little kid and didn't know how to drive. No matter what catastrophe you encountered when Mommy was driving, you had to trust her to handle it because you couldn't do anything about it. The same thing happens when you get on a plane; most of us don't even know what direction the plane is headed but we trust the pilot to get us to our destination. If we hit an air pocket and the plane starts to rock, all we can do is fasten our seatbelts and trust that the trained, experienced, qualified pilot will handle it. We don't go running up to the cockpit to give him directions because we wouldn't know what we were talking about and we would only be getting in the way.

Another example that comes to mind is trying to help in the kitchen when I was a little girl. I surely meant well but no matter what I was trying to do, I got in the way more than I got anything accomplished. We do the same thing with God when we step in there trying to help. We spill stuff and cause problems. We cut stuff wrong and create waste. We may even cause some minor accidents. The heart was in the right place and the intentions were good but I just wasn't the right person for the job. Much more would have been accomplished if I hadn't been there "getting in the way." Thankfully, experience is a great teacher and even though we may not get the message at first, eventually, after we have been through enough "stuff", we get it.

I wish I could say that now that I know that it's better to

submit and let God handle it that I always do that. Unfortunately, on occasion I still try to tell God what to do but now I catch myself when I do. The prayer I pray at these times is, "Lord, help me to get out of your way so that your will may be done. Help me to accept and follow your will even if I don't understand it because you have always taken care of me and you promise that you always will." I say to you, my sister, some of the "stuff" you are going through might be because you keep getting in God's way, telling Him what to do and how to do it. Get out of God's way and you will be amazed at what He will do.

SONGS:

Shirley Caesar:	Faith Moves God
Kirk Franklin:	He Can Handle It
Mississippi Mass Choir:	It Remains to be Seen
Cece Winans:	I Surrender All

GIVE LIGHT TO YOUR DREAMS

Recently I asked a lady in Spanish when she was due to give birth. My friend who was with me spoke a little Spanish and missed some of the exchange so she asked me why I had said something about light. Suddenly, it occurred to me that the literal translation of the Spanish term for giving birth, *dar luz,* is to give light. It hit me like "wow!" What a concept that when you give birth, you are actually giving light.

If we are honest with ourselves, we will admit that we have dreams and goals deep inside of us that have never seen the light of day. I know that I have a lot of fantasies that I have not shared with even my spouse or my closest friend. When I stop and take inventory of why I haven't shared them, I realize that I am afraid someone may think I am being unrealistic or just gone plain nuts. I guess there's the part of me that doesn't want to be judged or viewed differently from the rational image I usually project.

The biggest dream starts out as a small idea and sometimes it needs time to gestate and take shape before we can share it with others or act on it. However, if we keep it in the dark too long, it will eventually rot. Life holds very few guarantees and we have no assurance that the pursuit of our dream will result in success. However, if we never give it light, we have a 100% guarantee that it will not succeed.

Undoubtedly, there are many people who will be able to give you one hundred reasons why your dream won't work. If you listen to them, you will discard your idea like a used paper towel. On the other hand, if you can find just one person who shares your vision who will tell you to "go for it", I say seek out that person. Grandmothers are priceless in this role. They will tell you, "Go for it, baby", even if they have doubts, or they don't understand the mechanics of the dream. My grandmother realized that it was better for me to pursue a dream and have it fail than to spend time wallowing in regret and wondering about what might have been.

If we allow our dreams to die in the dark, we deprive ourselves of knowing just how much we are capable of accomplishing. In addition, we cheat the world of our special gifts. If we are satisfied to crawl around on the ground when we are capable of flying, then we do not deserve the benefits and rewards that come from flying.

It is quite possible that we will lay on our deathbeds thinking maybe we shouldn't have taken some of the paths we took in life. However, it is much more likely that we will spend our last moments contemplating and regretting the dreams we kept in the dark and the risks we never took. Most dreams are not age-dependent so as long as there is breath, there is always hope. If we want it badly enough, we can find the honest, ethical and God-centered means to achieve it.

God meant for us to have fulfilled lives but, He won't live our lives for us. We must be willing to seek His guidance, follow our calling and give birth to our dreams. We must lift the shadows of fear and doubt and let our lights shine through to the world around us. It can be very scary to take the big step of pursuing a dream and bringing it to fruition. For starters, we have no guarantee that it will work and there is always the fear that others will criticize and ridicule us. To all that, I say "so what?"

Remember that some of your biggest critics have no goals and no dreams and have never attempted anything on their own. Perhaps the real reason for their criticizing is to discourage you from going forward and possibly succeeding, thus leaving them behind. Don't let your dreams die in the dark because you are worried about what others think. You are the only you and you must do what you must do. With God on your side, you can accomplish all that you set your mind to do and when you do, don't forget to give Him credit.

SONGS:
This Little Light of Mine
McFadden and Whitehead: Ain't No Stopping Us Now
Cece Winans: Because of You

SCRIPTURE:
Neither do people light a lamp and put it under a bowl. Instead they put it on its stand and it gives light to everyone in the house.
Matthew 5:15

CHILDREN REALLY DO LIVE WHAT THEY LEARN

One day I called a friend of mine who wasn't feeling well to see how she was doing. Her two-year-old daughter was home with her and was making a ruckus in the background. I told my friend to put her daughter on the phone. I asked the little girl, "What are you doing, sweetie?" She said, "I am getting my bag; I am going to work." My friend and I started to laugh hysterically but in that moment we both realized what an impact adults have on children and how the lives we live are the greatest lessons that our children will learn.

I said to my friend, "Girl, you know she's telling you this is how she sees you. Suppose you were sitting around doing something immoral or illegal. She would call you out." We don't have to be biological parents to be parents to the children in our lives. To this day, I remember every time an adult encouraged me with my dreams and I probably remember even more strongly every time an adult said a cruel, unkind or discouraging word to me.

Children really are blank slates and everything we throw at them leaves a mark, so we really need to be careful what we contribute to their lives. I don't have children of my own, but I have a whole bunch of children I love as if they were my own. At this point, the most important thing to me is for those children to say, "You know, Ms. Jetola really believed in me and encouraged me." A kind encouraging word to a child takes so little and has such a lasting impact that we have no choice but to

113

take the time to do it.

I think the most important message we must give our children is that they are valuable to us. This value is measured more by how we treat them than by what we say to them. Think about it! When you go into a store, the valuable merchandise is displayed under lock and key. This tells you that the merchant places high esteem on these products. The five-dollar rings may be in a basket on the counter but, you better believe that the expensive stuff in locked up and they will only show you one piece at a time, "for insurance purposes." Now think of your children as your favorite ring or bracelet and how you would treat it. Where would you leave it? Who would you allow to take care of it. Does it compute?

Even when children can't talk very well or read or write, they are conscious of how much value we bestow on them. Are we willing to spend time with them? Do we really listen to them? Do we praise them? Do we encourage them? Do we give them encouragement for their accomplishments? Every now and then we need to check ourselves because sometimes we do and say things unconsciously and we are making big imprints on the little souls. Whatever our real value systems may be, children are going to pick up on it because it will be determined by what we do more than by what we say.

The message we want our children to hear is that they are OK and we value them just the way they are. If a child grows up thinking (s)he's never enough and what (s)he does is never enough, it kills their spirit a little piece at a time. No loving mama wants to be a spirit killer but if we don't pay attention, that is exactly what will happen. Every now and then, you need to pump the brakes and take stock of what you are giving off because verily it will come back to you and you will be surprised.

You probably haven't thought about it but take a moment to think back to when you were in the third grade. What messages do you remember from the adults in your life? What did grandma tell you? What did your teacher say to you? What did Sister Johnson at church say? How did it make you feel? How did you react? Close your eyes and picture yourself as a little girl. Fast forward to today—can you identify elements of your thoughts and behaviors that have been influenced by those messages you got as a child? Hah! When I did this exercise for the first time, it was so real that I cried.

Children are precious cargo and we must handle them with care because the damage we do today will echo for generations to come. Each of us must do our part to make the world a healthier, safer and better place for them. Let us not sit around grumbling about what's wrong with the children and the world and do nothing about it. If we can identify the problem, we can also devise solutions.

SONGS:

Yolanda Adams: What About the Children?

George Benson: The Greatest Love of All

Stevie Wonder: You Are the Sunshine of my Life

BOOK:

Eric Copage: Black Pearls For Parents

SCRIPTURE:

Sons are a heritage from the Lord, children a reward from him. Like arrows in the hands of a warrior are sons born in one's youth. Blessed is the man whose quiver is full of them. They will not be put to shame when they contend with their enemies at the gate.
Psalms 127: 2-5

Let the little children come to me and do not hinder them, for the kingdom of God belongs to such as these. Luke 18:16

116

WAVE BYE, BYE

I think that sometimes we become so excited about learning to drive that we overlook some of the advantages we give up as passengers. For example, when something interests us as we drive along, as drivers, we do not have the luxury of turning around and staring to satisfy our curiosity. However, as passengers we can turn around and stare and marvel until the object of our attention is out of sight. The wonder of such an experience is that as we move forward the things we leave behind become smaller and smaller. Sometimes we give ourselves whiplash trying to stare at what we are leaving behind when what we really need to do is to wave bye, bye.

Our lives, like nature, are a series of seasons. Events and individuals come into our lives for a season and when the time comes to move on, it is healthiest and best to leave without tears, remorse or regret. When I got laid off from my job, I made a conscious decision that I would not cling, cry or hold on. I was at the company for four and a half years and gave my best. When they decided they no longer had need of my services, I ran forward to the future with my arms open to embrace whatever God had in store for me. I told myself the season of that place was over and I needed to put my mind in the right frame to move on. Besides, I had always wanted to write but could never seem to find the time in the past. Now I have the blessing of unlimited writing time and I give praise.

Sometimes we think God has taken something away from us and we question why. One of the lessons I have learned on my journey is that God does not take anything away from us.

117

Instead he positions us in the right lane to make the next turn He
has in store for us. Picture yourself driving along on a four-lane
highway. You are just zipping along in the fast lane (lane number
1) but you have to make a right exit about a mile up the road.
You know that you will need to get into the slow lane (lane 4)
in order to make the exit. As pleasant as things are in lane 1, if
you don't reposition yourself, you will not be able to exit when
you need to do so. Consequently, you will delay your arrival to
your destination or you may not be able to get there at all.

I think the highway is a fitting metaphor for life and many of
the life's object lessons are aptly demonstrated from the vantage
point of the car. Often the very thing that we think God has
taken away from us is mutually exclusive to the better plan He
has in mind for us. We cannot make our exit to success from
the wrong lane. Sometimes we know this but we think we can
control the timing and we mess things up. Timing is a critical
part of driving and of life and sometimes God has to change our
lane before we are ready so that we will avoid the pile-up ahead
of us.

When we become repositioned, the view changes because
we are farther from where we were. As we look back, the
objects left behind become smaller and eventually fade from
view. I say wave bye, bye and start looking ahead. New scenery
will come into view but we cannot exercise the proper
appreciation if we aren't looking ahead. It doesn't matter if we
are just catching a peek in the rearview mirror or if we have
completely turned around to gaze behind us. We will miss the
view before us and that would be cheating ourselves of what's in
store.

It is hard to say goodbye, especially when we are unsure of

the future, but we must learn to treat life as an adventure. We know that what lies ahead will either be similar, worse or better. To me, that makes the effort worth it. It's better to go forward with an open mind than to wonder forever what might have been.

SCRIPTURE:

...the old things are passed away. Behold all things are become new.
2 Corinthians 5:17 KJV

Jetola E. Anderson-Blair

METAMORPHOSIS

There are so many lessons to be learned in nature about growth and renewal. Think of how the trees have to shed their old leaves to make room for the new ones. Think of how snakes and other reptiles shed their old skin so the new ones can come out. Think of how baby chicks lose the soft, pretty, yellow down when they grow into big chickens. Most fascinating of all, think of how the caterpillar has to completely give up its existing life in order to become the beautiful butterfly it was intended to be. When I see these changes happening, the thought that usually crosses my mind is, "Whew, that must hurt." and I am sure I am right. That's how it is with life also; becoming what we were meant to be means shedding some old parts of ourselves and that can to be a painful process.

Sometimes the shedding process includes our belief systems, people we used to hang out with, places we used to go and our self-talk. I imagine that the new "skin" is probably quite tender and vulnerable but it's all part of the process. There can't be too many life events that hurt as much as having to make the decision to rid your life of certain people. If you're going to grow and make progress, you will have to leave some of the people in your life behind. Every one of us has that one person who sees the negative in every situation and always pours cold water on our dreams. If you plan to take wings, you have to discard the person who's always focusing on your failures and always telling you that you are crazy and that can't do it, whatever "it" might be. It is good to have wind beneath our wings but glue in our wings is a whole other matter.

Unfortunately, sometimes we are our own worst enemies

thinking negatively and discouraging ourselves. We just may have to shed the negative self-talk and become like that little engine we learned about as children telling ourselves "I think I can; I think I can." Whatever we plant in our minds ultimately becomes imprinted there so we must control input. When we truly start to press towards the mark, we will also fully believe the promise from Philippians 4:13, "I can do all things through Christ who strengthens me." The two ways of thinking are mutually exclusive and one will have to flee from our minds. The choice is ours — can or can't?

As we shed the old thoughts, people, places, etc., we may feel a little out of equilibrium at first, but each small victory will strengthen us and boost our confidence. From time to time, we may even slip back, but as we grow and taste the rewards of our metamorphosis, we'll find that we can't stay in the old place. It will become less comfortable. Think of the snake trying to crawl back into the old skin—not a pretty picture is it? The process of becoming the best possible you means that you have to discard the old you and move forward.

The new you will have the confidence to take worthwhile risks and reap the rewards. Your path will not be directed by others, but by God. You will care less about what others think and their approval or disapproval will matter little, if at all. You will learn the lessons from your bumps in the road and move on to your next endeavor with a wiser perspective. You will have a greater sense of what truly makes you happy, as opposed to what is supposed to make you happy. You will trust your instincts more and believe in yourself. You will become far more interesting and enjoy your own company more, as will others. Today you are simply the raw material for all that you can be.

Your metamorphosis will be the manufacturing process which converts you into your best self.

The funny thing is that some people will be appalled by the new you. But if you stop and examine the situation closely, you will find that the people who are most dissatisfied with the new you will be the people who were wallowing in negativity with you "back in the day." The others will be the dream stealers who poked holes in every idea you ever had. Because their opinions do not matter to the new you and you follow your dreams anyway, they will be confounded. Oh well, that's their problem—not yours. If you still think the way you did ten years ago, then you have not grown and your new skin has not emerged yet.

SONGS:

Walter Hawkins:	Changed
Jennifer Holiday:	I Am Changing
Shun Pace-Rhodes:	I Know I've Been Changed
Cece Winans:	Because of You

SCRIPTURE: *When I was a child, I thought like a child.*
I Corinthians 13:11

COMPARED TO WHAT?

If you look in any phone book in any city, you will find countless businesses with the name "Superior." From third grade English grammar we remember that "superior" implies comparison to something else and being deemed better. Now, let us be real. Is every business that touts itself as "superior" really living up to its implied promise? I would bet that a quick check with the Better Business Bureau would yield quite a few with less than stellar records. This reminds us of the need to have our eyes open and to evaluate everything that comes into our lives. The Bible tells us to test them to see what they are made of. However, sometimes we get so excited by the glitter of the wrapping paper that we do not truly examine the content of the package.

Sometimes it's a job opportunity, a potential mate or a deal of a lifetime. Somehow we manage to convince ourselves that is indeed superior but in the words of Ray Charles, we must ask ourselves, "Compared to what?" What are we using as the measuring standard? Are we just caught up in appearance and the moment? Oftentimes we do not evaluate the things which come into our lives and we accept them blindly. When pressure is applied and the glass breaks, we are actually surprised to find that what we thought was a diamond was nothing but glass.

Too often we underestimate our power. In the right frame of mind and with God's guidance, we can discern a lot of inferior situations masquerading as "superior." Much of the craziness that happens in our lives is a result of our failure to separate the wheat from the shaft and making decisions accordingly. We need some established standards to use as evaluation tools to help us determine what is actually for our good versus what just seems good for us.

It is usually a bad strategy to jump first and then sort out the mess later or to buy based on the label without examining the merchandise. Unfortunately, too often that is exactly what we do. We fall for the "superior" label; accept it at face value and then we are disappointed when reality doesn't match our preconceived perception.

It is not anyone else's responsibility to discern for us. When we are grown and responsible, we need to think for ourselves. After all, that's what being grown up is all about. Making bad decisions is a part of the game of life and part of learning and growing. However, we have to hold ourselves accountable and let go of the weak excuses.

I know that in my own case, most of my drama could have been prevented by spending more time evaluating circumstances and making meaningful comparisons and arriving at better decisions. However, when the waves of pressure start to rise, it's difficult to think clearly. Those are the times when we need prayer the most. Sometimes we are too overwhelmed to even pray for ourselves and we need to reach out and ask someone to pray on our behalf. When we seek God's direction in our decision-making, we are more insightful and are not easily fooled by labels.

SONGS:

Andrae Crouch: We Need To Hear From You
GMWA Women of Worship: Order My Steps

124

GIVE THANKS ANYWAY

For some unknown reason we have convinced ourselves that our lives should be problem free or our occasional problems should be short-lived. I am not sure why we think this way, maybe it from watching too much television—the crisis is usually solved in twenty-five minutes. Whatever the reason may be, reality is that all our lives will be seasoned with our fair share of problems. The only distinction we can look forward to is our reaction to the trials in our lives.

Some people naturally see the glass as half-full while others can only see the emptiness. When life is going smoothly, it is easy for everyone to project a spirit of gratitude. However, when life's hurricanes come along and hurl us against the rocks and leave us wounded and bleeding, the half-empty people will only be able to identify and complain about what's wrong, what's missing or what's out of place.

On the other hand, the half-full people will find something positive in even the most horrific situation and manage to give thanks anyway. For the most part, I try to be a half-full person and maintain an attitude of gratitude. However, I am ashamed to admit that there are times when I allow trifling, silly matters to throw me off course. I may indulge in self-pity for a while but I am never comfortable there. Soon I am overcome with guilt and I feel compelled to search for the good in my circumstances.

I realize that being able to smile and give thanks in any circumstance is a special blessing and I thank God for that gift. People do not expect us to be OK when trouble comes into our lives. However, if we have the presence of mind to turn to the hills for our strength, we will be able to withstand the pain and heartaches which come with trouble. When we should be falling apart, we will be jumping for joy and giving thanks despite our circumstances. That kind of behavior will confound half-empty people but we shouldn't let that deter us. They just may learn something!

Our greatest challenge is to learn to be content no matter what our situation may be and to stand firmly in our knowledge that our times are in God's hands. We may not always understand what's going on in our lives but we should give thanks anyway. Gratitude builds on itself. When we are focused on finding the good and giving thanks, the good starts to grow. Our outlook changes because we can't complain and express gratitude at the same time.

Sometimes we stare in wonder when we see other people undergoing major trials in their lives. We are not able to conceive how we would ever survive in similar situations. I think anyone would become overwhelmed by the reality of major catastrophes. However, the real survivors who set wonderful examples for us are the individuals who are able to keep their eyes focused on the positive. By not dwelling on the negative, they lessen its impact. When we concentrate on the negative, we will start to sink. For this reason, we must give thanks anyway and remain encouraged no matter what life throws our way.

BOOK:
Joan Lunden: A Bend In The Road Is Not The End of The Road

SONGS:
Rev. James Cleveland:	It's Been a Good Day
Walter Hawkins:	Be Grateful
L. A. Mass Choir:	That's When You Bless Me

SCRIPTURE:
I know what it is to be in need, and I know what it is to have plenty. I have learned the secret of being content in any and every situation. Philippians 4: 12

Jetola E. Anderson-Blair

IT'S NOT THE DETAIL JOB; IT'S THE DETAILS

Recently, I had my car detailed and it sparkled like new. Now, you know that there is nothing that feels like a sparkling clean car on a sunny day. I had that magnolia air freshener going and all was well with my world. I noticed the looks my car got at stop signs and stop lights. People couldn't help but stare because the car looked good. About three days into my reverie, I was driving along with the sunroof open and Dianne Reeves crooning when all of a sudden the car started making funny sounds and shifting to the right. I turned down the music so I could hear better and no, it wasn't my imagination—pretty girl was surely making crazy sounds. Thankfully, I was close enough to my mechanic's shop that I managed to say a little prayer, slow down and crawl there. I can't even remember everything that was wrong, but I know it ended up costing a lot of money. I should have known it was going to be bad since even I could tell that there was something wrong.

It's amazing how many times in our lives we become so infatuated with the detail job that we overlook important details. I know that on many occasions I have overlooked critical details because they were at odds with the image I had emblazoned on my mind. Sometimes there was something that was just a little "off" about a situation—a person, a job, etc. However, instead of following my instincts, I chose to ignore that little voice saying, "Pay attention to the details." and focused on the detail job. The high gloss of the body and the shine of the tires left me thinking that nothing was wrong, but I am telling you, it's that under-the-hood activity that will trip you up every time.

Life is about growth and growth comes from learning from our mistakes and avoiding them the next time around. However, we can only learn by paying attention and studying. The lessons we need to learn are often right before our eyes but we often overlook them because we are distracted by other factors which don't matter nearly as much. Our ability to see and learn is heavily influenced by our thoughts and spiritual state.

We can often become blinded by the superficial and make decisions that reflect our lack of vision. If we are driven by the detail job and the critical mechanical and electrical matters are not in right order, the potential of a breakdown is intensified. What's the point of the high gloss to our lives if there is no inward satisfaction?

We often make the best decisions we know, but if we don't seek God's guidance, our decisions will come up short and the long term results will reflect the deficiency. As we grow spiritually and develop a personal relationship with God, it will become natural to seek His guidance in our decision-making processes. When our paths are directed by God, we will be less likely to be drawn by the detail job. We will experience the feeling of real growth when our focus shifts to the meaningful details.

SONGS:
GMWA Women of Worship: Order My Steps
Tremaine Hawkins: What Shall I Do Lord?

SCRIPTURE:
Trust in the Lord with all your heart and lean not on your own understanding; In all your ways acknowledge Him, and He will make your paths straight. Proverbs 3:5-6

BEND, DON'T BREAK

It is inevitable that strong winds will blow in our lives and they will take many forms – health problems, financial challenges, job loss, wayward children, etc. In Texas we often get severe weather warnings for hurricanes, storms, flash floods, tornadoes, etc. With a bit of preparation we can feel a little better but never totally confident that we can handle the storms. However, we usually don't get any warnings when life's storms are about to strike. They often hit really fast and furiously and we are often caught off guard. Nevertheless, it is amazing how two individuals will be hit with seemingly similar situations but end up with totally different results. The difference is often that one person bends and the other breaks.

When storms hit our lives, instead of wallowing in self-pity and trying to figure out "why me?", it's best to accept the situation and try to figure out how we're going to solve the matter. Resisting the change and the storm will take more energy than adjusting to it and will yield less effective results. If you watch trees in a storm, you will realize that the branches that bend with the wind may dance around and rock but they do not break. On the other hand, the branches that resist and don't bend will eventually rip and shred. It's a simple law of nature and things are no different for us.

God gives us a great reserve of courage and we really do have all we need. However, we often don't recognize this and we try to solve our circumstances by ourselves. Our own strength is not sufficient to withstand the storms which will undoubtedly come into our lives. Our natural reaction is to cling to and try to maintain the status quo. By doing so, we develop a certain rigidity which makes us prime candidates for breaking. When we struggle on our own and try to take matters into our own hands, we are at the mercy of the elements.

God really does have our best interest at heart but we may not remember this when we are getting whipped from all sides. As scary as it may seem, the answer is total surrender. Instead of fighting the storms, it is best to relinquish our situation to God and trust that He can handle it much better than we ever could. His strength will provide us with the flexibility to bend and go with the flow, no matter what's going on in our lives. The choice is ours to make. Will we bend or will we break?

SONGS:

Shirley Caesar: He's Working It Out
GMWA Mass Choir: Bend, Don't Break
Betty Griffin Keller: You Can Make It
Donald Malloy: Everything Will Be Alright

BOOK:

Suzan D. Johnson Cook: Too Blessed To Be Stressed

SCRIPTURE:

I have loved you with an everlasting love; I have drawn you with loving-kindness. Jeremiah 31:3

Blessed are the poor in spirit, for theirs is the kingdom of heaven. Matthew 5:3

ORDER FORM

In My Sister's Shoes,
Essays of Inspiration and Encouragement For Women

To order your copy of *In My Sister's Shoes* please submit your request with payment to the publisher:

Cross Keys Publishing
PO Box 752026
Houston, TX 77275
Web site: http://www.pageturner.net/crosskeys

(Print or Type)

Name:---

Address:---

City:----------------------------State------Zip----------

My order for *In My Sister's Shoes* is as follows:

-------Copies @ $10.00:-------------

8 ¼% TX Sales Tax (.83 ea.)-------------

Shipping and Handling ($2.50 ea.).------------

Total:-----------

ORDER FORM

In My Sister's Shoes,
Essays of Inspiration and Encouragement For Women

To order your copy of *In My Sister's Shoes* please
submit your request with payment to the publisher:

Cross Keys Publishing
PO Box 752026
Houston, TX 77275
Web site: http://www.pageturner.net/crosskeys

(Print or Type)

Name:--

Address:--

City:----------------------------State------Zip----------

My order for *In My Sister's Shoes* is as follows:

-------Copies @ $10.00:-------------

8 ¼% TX Sales Tax (.83 ea.)-------------

Shipping and Handling ($2.50 ea.).------------

Total:------------